KT-169-465

Acclaim

Marion Dowling, Vice President, Early Education
A beautiful book that comes to the UK at just the right time.
It is essential reading for all who are privileged to live and
work with children. Arnold presents many issues but his
closing message resonates most strongly: Children gather
memories from their earliest years which remain with them,
and adults who respect and love children will ensure that
they amass a bank of positive memories which shine through
and sustain them throughout their lives.

Anand Shukla, Chief Executive, Family and Childcare Trust
It's all-too-rare to read something so beautifully written,
distilling a lifetime's reflection and experience. On every
page, there is something which will resonate with every
parent, carer and teacher. Often challenging, occasionally
provocative, always stimulating and uplifting, *Their Name Is
Today* is a joyous description of childhood, and at its heart,
an acclamation of family life.

Tricia David, Professor Emeritus of Education,
Canterbury Christ Church University
Today, when reports of turmoil, violence, and abuses of power
fill the news, Arnold's work is a beacon of hope calling us to
remember to be respectful and reverential, to grow a world in
which all children are truly loved and their parents thought-
fully supported. *Their Name Is Today* should be required
reading for teachers and policymakers everywhere.

Betty Williams, Nobel Laureate
A gentle book with a powerful punch and a clear message.
Listen to your children; they have a lot to say.

John Coe, chair, National Association for Primary Education
A wonderful book which all parents and teachers should read. Full of insights into the growth of children and never sentimental but always touching the heart. The pages are packed with truth and it is best not to read too much on a single occasion. One chapter at a time will give more opportunity for reflection and an unspoken dialogue between Arnold and his readers.

Clive Ireson, director, Association of Christian Teachers
This timely book reminds us that children need time to explore, investigate and above all be allowed to play. Every child needs to know they are loved. Arnold is right in stressing the need for childhood to be a time of enjoyment and fascination. I urge you to read the book, share it with your friends and colleagues and be brave enough to implement it allowing all our children to reach their full potential in a loving, caring environment.

Barry Carpenter OBE, international education consultant
There is no greater challenge for twenty-first century society than how it treasures childhood and nurtures its children. This timely book offers insight and inspiration on how this universal goal might be achieved.

Jonathan Kozol, author, *Amazing Grace*
Beautiful . . . it is Arnold's reverence for children that I love.

Joan Almon, co-founder, Alliance for Childhood
Arnold writes with deep insight, reminding us of the meaning of childhood and the need to protect it for the sake of the children and all of humanity. His tone is beautiful, warm, and supportive. The passages from parents and teachers add a great deal.

Their Name Is Today

Other books by Johann Christoph Arnold

Why Forgive?
Why Children Matter
Sex, God, and Marriage
Be Not Afraid
Seeking Peace
Rich in Years
Cries from the Heart

www.plough.com

Their Name Is Today

*Reclaiming Childhood
in a Hostile World*

Johann Christoph Arnold

Foreword by Mark K. Shriver

Plough Publishing House

Published by Plough Publishing House
Walden, New York
Robertsbridge, England
Elsmore, Australia
www.plough.com

Cover image: Copyright © Corbis Images

ISBN 13: 978-0-87486-612-4

USA Printing 1, Aug. 2014: 30,000	UK printing 1, Aug. 2014: 5,000
USA Printing 2, Aug. 2014: 30,000	UK printing 2, Aug. 2014: 15,000
	UK printing 3, Aug. 2014: 15,000
	UK printing 3, Aug. 2014: 50,000

Their Name Is Today is based on Arnold's acclaimed book *Endangered: Your Child in a Hostile World* (Plough, 2000). The author has extensively revised, expanded, and updated the text with new stories and topics to address the sweeping changes that have taken place since then.

In several instances, names have been changed to protect the contributors' privacy.

A catalog record for this book is available from the British Library.

Printed and bound by CPI Group (UK) Ltd, Croydon, CR0 4YY

We are guilty of many errors and many faults,
but our worst crime is abandoning the children,
    neglecting the fountain of life.
Many things can wait. Children cannot.
Right now their bones are being formed,
    their blood is being made,
    and their senses are being developed.
To them we cannot answer, "Tomorrow."
    Their name is today.

Gabriela Mistral
NOBEL LAUREATE

Contents

Foreword

I bet this is the shortest foreword you will ever read!
Why?

Because I do not want to delay you more than a
minute or two from reading my good friend Johann
Christoph Arnold's book.

It really is that good.

Like Christoph, I have had the honor of working
with children of all ages throughout my career.
During college summer breaks I tutored troubled
inner-city high school students. After college, I
created a program that works with juvenile delin-
quents in Baltimore. In the Maryland Legislature, as
the first chair of the Joint Committee on Children,
Youth and Families, I collaborated with national
and international experts on child development and
passed legislation designed to help young children
enter kindergarten ready to learn. For the last twelve
years, I have had the privilege of working at Save the
Children, giving kids around the world a healthy start,

opportunities to learn, and protection from harm, because children deserve a childhood.

On the home front, my wife, Jeanne, and I have been married for twenty-two years and have been blessed with three children: Molly, 16, Tommy, 14, and Emma, 9.

Like you, we have struggled with many of the issues that Christoph addresses in this marvelous book, from the impact of electronics, to academic pressures, to the lack of unstructured play time, to the violence and poverty that children face daily.

Jeanne and I often find ourselves discussing how to deal with these very issues as we raise our own children. Things are coming at us so fast and furiously, it's overwhelming. We have tried to do the right thing, making numerous changes as our kids grow.

I only wish that Christoph had written this book seventeen years ago, before Jeanne and I became parents! He could have helped us on the child-rearing front, in the political arena, and on the job.

The stories Christoph shares have helped Jeanne and me as we interact with our children and their friends, and I am confident that they will help you in your home, in your classroom, and in your neighborhood.

If you want to glean insights into how to raise and influence children to be more compassionate and considerate, more courageous and confident, more independent, secure, and unselfish; if you want your children to be more loving and joy-filled, then get reading!

And share this book. I've already shared my dog-eared manuscript with several friends. They responded as I did. One replied: "It makes me want to go back and do a few things differently for my own children. . . ."

I have written too much. Read on and learn from a wise friend who loves and reveres children, whose words can help us all, whatever our age, to give and receive joy.

Mark K. Shriver
President, Save the Children Action Network
Author, A Good Man: Rediscovering My Father, Sargent Shriver

Preface

It's high time for a hopeful book about childhood. We live in difficult times and many people have lost their joy in life. But whenever we feel discouraged, all we need to do is look at children. They are among the most vulnerable in today's fast-paced culture, yet their trust in us and their irrepressible enthusiasm should always inspire us to keep going.

There are more than enough books about education and parenting – books with gloomy statistics and dire warnings for the future of our society and its children.

Yet there are many reasons for hope. Across America and around the world, there are people who care passionately about children. But they often feel overwhelmed, fighting lonely battles for what they know to be right and true. In this book, I want to bring their voices together so their valuable insights and courageous examples can be shared.

This book is dedicated first and foremost to all children, wherever they live. It is also dedicated to the parents and teachers who care for them day and night. To me, these people are the true heroes, on the front lines every day, facing difficult odds.

We all need to become advocates for children, parents, and teachers, encouraging them whenever we can, and finding ways to make their lives a little easier.

A book can't change the world. But parents and teachers can – by loving each child entrusted to them. That's why this book is in your hands. I hope it will encourage and invigorate you to hear from others who have children of their own or work with them every day, and who share your passion and commitment.

The wisdom collected in these pages is rooted in the realities of daily life. That's what gives me hope. Because no matter how dark the horizon seems, we must never forget that for us, as for children, the chance for a new beginning starts every morning.

Johann Christoph Arnold
Rifton, New York

Chapter 1

The World Needs Children

If we do not keep on speaking terms with children, we become merely machines for eating and earning money.

JOHN UPDIKE

The cry of a newborn baby catches at the heart. It says, "Love me. Help me. Protect me." As adults, we consider ourselves the helpers and protectors. But the more I think about it, the more I'm convinced that we need children more than they need us.

Experts inform us that overpopulation is destroying the earth. I disagree: greed and selfishness are ruining the planet, not children. They are born givers, not takers. They are also born teachers, if we are wise enough to hear the truths they bring. In the midst of our complex adult lives, we must make time to take in the lessons that only children can teach.

Children demand honesty and simplicity. They expect words to line up with deeds. Though children can quickly get angry, they forgive just as fast, giving others the great gift of a second chance. They have a strong sense of justice and fair play. They look at everything with new eyes, and point out to us the incredible beauty of the world around us.

Imagine what would happen if we applied these values to our government, foreign policy, corporate business models, environmental decisions, and educational theory.

A society that doesn't welcome children is doomed. Yet the odds don't appear to be stacked in favor of children or their caregivers, whether parents or teachers. As the gap between rich and poor steadily widens, more and more families can hardly afford basics like housing and insurance. In many cities, desperate family conditions have necessitated the rise of twenty-four-hour childcare. Parents who work long hours have no choice but to yield their children to caregivers who must take over many traditional parenting tasks such as dressing the children, providing breakfast, caring for them through sickness, and tucking them in at night.

Meanwhile, new and untested political mandates that threaten children's originality and abilities are handed down to teachers and students. Voices of opposition rarely reach the ears of those who drive these decisions.

Beverly Braxton, a retired teacher and parenting consultant, has worked on behalf of children for decades. She sums up our current dilemma:

> I ask people in my community what concerns them most about children growing up in today's world. Most people list similar concerns: the amount of time spent on media and technology, children's exposure to sexual content and violence, lack of family time and eating on the run, the stress related to academic excellence, and children becoming less interested in spending time exploring the outdoors. Yet, when asked if they have any ideas regarding how these issues might be addressed, everyone I speak to seems to shrug their shoulders in exasperation.

Resignation may be an understandable response to this tangle of evils. But it is not the only response. If all of these concerns seem too great to tackle at once, at least each of us can start with the children we encounter every day.

My wife, Verena, and I both grew up in large families and were blessed with eight children of our own. God gave us forty-four grandchildren and, so far, one great-grandchild. We are thankful for each one of them.

During our marriage of almost fifty years, we have traveled together all over the globe. We have spent time in many developing countries as well as in war zones such as Rwanda, Iraq, Gaza, and Northern Ireland during "The Troubles." On each of these journeys, we met hundreds of children. In their schools, we saw great determination despite very little funding. With eyes full of eagerness, these students showed us what they were learning, sang songs, and made us feel welcome. Some had walked miles for the privilege of an education. The hunger and hardship that many had endured was not yet written in their faces.

We saw that in some of the most impoverished nations, children are considered a national treasure. They represent the future of an entire civilization, not only the inheritors of a family name. Even some of the most destitute villages had a school in a central location, raised by community effort and whatever meager materials could be scraped together.

Every time we returned to America, we experienced a culture shock. Western society is fueled by money, but relatively little finds its way into child-care centers and schools. Are places of learning the center of community life? Are children considered a national treasure? In terms of future income earners with buying power, yes. But as unique individuals who offer hope for the renewal of civilization? Not so much. In fact, often the discussion centers on the pros and cons of having children at all: the financial risks, the unaffordable health costs, and the burden of education.

When I spoke with my neighbors Steve and Shannon, who have four children, about this tendency to view children in economic terms, Shannon answered decisively:

> Unfortunately when the media and the surrounding world tells us, "A child costs this much money," that puts a lot of stress on people. You have to say, "How much love can I give?" not, "How much money do I have?"
>
> Most parents, when they see their baby for the first time, can't say, "Take him back," or "I don't want her." I would be hard-pressed to find a parent who doesn't look into the eyes of a child and feel an instant love, an overwhelming sense of joy.

What good is it to be happy if you don't have someone to share it with? Is it possible to have joy by yourself – selfish joy? It's meant to be given away; the more kids you have, the more joy there is to spread around and amplify it.

Despite what the "child-free" movement would have us believe, having children today is normal, good, and natural. Parenting should not be viewed as an insurmountable financial risk or a great emotional and psychological burden. It is not something for experts only. But it *does* need a heart of love for children and a willingness to sacrifice for them. Without the readiness for sacrifice, how can we experience what life is all about?

Of course, there are many people who are all too familiar with sacrifice, working in difficult circumstances or dangerous jobs with little reward. You might expect them to argue that in a hazardous, frightening world it is simply too hard to protect someone as helpless as a child. But a recent conversation I had with a young police officer challenges that assumption, too.

Among my various pastoral duties, I serve as chaplain for several state and local law enforcement agencies. This gives me the chance to join them in serving those in need around my county and state. Mark, one of the officers I counsel, was involved in a serious altercation with a troubled young man who had outstanding warrants for his arrest. While attempting to bring him into custody, the situation became violent.

During post-incident counseling, Mark shared with me how profoundly this experience had affected him. He and his fiancée, Rita, reevaluated their priorities and decided to marry a year earlier than planned. In fact, I was honored to offer a prayer of blessing at their marriage, and later to bless the arrival of their son. Mark shared his thoughts about parenting:

> We always thought about having kids. Our main fear was for their future. Will they live in a world of chaos, unable to enjoy growing up, always in fear for their lives? What will the survival rate be in the future? We realized that we need to raise kids with the right morals and attitude – "soldiers of tomorrow." It's up to us to raise our kids to be what we want the world to be. My contribution to tomorrow is to teach my son values like the difference between right and wrong. As scary as it is with the world going to hell, at least I can do something for one person.

We're not going to be here forever. We have to pass on what we can, because otherwise it stops here. I learned a lot from my grandfather. He would be upset if all the knowledge and life lessons that he shared ended with me. So I feel relieved that I get to pass it on to another generation. My son can take it on and hopefully pass it on to his kids.

Parenting is a roller-coaster ride. It's not always easy, but it's not always going to be tough either. The rewards compensate for the costs that you pay. The things that are given back to you far outweigh the "burden" of not being able to go out to the bar for a drink, or whatever you want to do. Nothing beats the feeling of their arms around you. Just to look a child in the eye and know that you're the reason they're here, to see them explore the world – you can't put that kind of feeling into words. Part of me that was locked away for many years is coming back out and I'm learning how to play like a child again.

I deal with harsh realities every day. To come home at night and just sit there and watch my son sleep – it makes the world okay.

Sceptics will say that it's one thing for a family with two parents and two jobs to talk about welcoming children. But I heard the same message from someone with none of these benefits. Lisa, a home-care nurse, raised her daughter alone.

My friends keep asking me how I did it. I'm still not sure how to answer. I could say it was tough. I could tell you that we ate whenever we had something to eat, and it was sometimes once a day. I could tell about sharing a mattress in front of the faulty heating element. But my daughter, who is nineteen now, will tell a different story: how we laughed till we knocked the heater over, how we cried onto each other's shoulders. Of course she would have liked a dad. Of course I kept praying for him, and he didn't come back. But where would I be without her? I don't think I would have made it alone. And I hate to think of the world without her in it.

Not every child is as fortunate as Lisa's daughter, raised by a brave and resourceful mother, or Mark's son, with two strong and determined parents in a secure home. But I've found that children remain children at heart, even those who have been deprived of a childhood. They may be victims of abuse, addictions, or broken families. Though emotionally scarred, they look at you with so much hope. You can see the questions in their eyes: "What can you do for me? Where do I fit into this world?" Over the years I have learned that every child has a story to tell. Each of their stories needs to be told to someone who has time to listen – a parent, a trusted teacher, a guidance counselor.

My wife and I are co-founders of a program called Breaking the Cycle, which seeks to bring the positive answer of nonviolent conflict resolution and forgiveness to schools, where the fear of school shootings, as well as gang violence and bullying, affects children, teachers, and parents. At some assemblies, we address several thousand students at once. Looking out over such a sea of children's faces is inspiring, but also sobering. Every assembly reminds me of the Hasidic saying, "If you save one child, you save the world." It is vital to tell children that they are important; that we are here for them and love them.

Hashim Garrett has become a keynote speaker in this program. At age fifteen, he was shot six times in a gang-related attack that left him partially paralyzed from the waist down. At first, he was filled with anger and a desire for revenge. But in time, he realized that forgiving the perpetrator would liberate him from the trap of hate, and give him the opportunity to help others.

A devout Muslim, Hashim says his faith has guided him toward forgiveness. It has also helped him and his wife make critical choices on the home front as they wrestle with the difficulties of raising a family responsibly:

I am blessed to have a beautiful wife, Mia, and two wonderful children. Being a husband with a disability is a test. There are things that I cannot do with my wife and children. I cannot play in the ocean with my children on vacation. I cannot teach them how to ride a bike. But my children know that their father loves them very much. I have learned that the quantity of our possessions is not what's truly important; it's the quality of time we spend together. When I am home, I play with them, hug them, bathe them, feed them, read with them, and most importantly, we pray together.

When we enrolled our two-year-old daughter in daycare, it was with an overwhelming sense of vulnerability; for the first time, we would leave our only child in the care of strangers. It seemed totally unavoidable. Harmony attended daycare nine hours a day while I worked and Mia went to school. After a time, we began to notice behavior and personality changes in Harmony. She would cry, throw tantrums, and not want to go to school in the morning. This was not the daughter we knew.

My wife seriously considered quitting her training to stay home with Harmony. At first, I was very concerned about Harmony's social development and our lack of teaching experience. I could just imagine our relatives and friends asking, "Why would you want to take your child out of childcare?" Then there was the financial sacrifice required for one parent to remain home, while the other worked full-time.

But it came to a tipping point. With our family spending most of our day away from one another, we were using our physical and emotional reserves on things other than our family. We missed the laughter in our home. We finally decided to begin home-schooling Harmony.

Our decision has transformed our home into a place where everyone is learning. My wife and I learn patience with our children. We learn to love, laugh, and appreciate the small things. We learn to forgive one another.

Hashim and Mia considered all the difficulties arrayed against them: Hashim's disability, their economic challenges, and their children's needs. Then they consciously chose to put their children first. To them, nothing was as important as those first precious years of being together and starting off right.

President Franklin D. Roosevelt often emphasized this essential task of families in society:

We all recognize that the spirit within the home is the most important influence in the growth of the child. In family life the child should first learn confidence in his own powers, respect for the feelings and the rights of others, the feeling of security and mutual good will, and faith in God. Mothers and fathers, by the kind of life they build within the four walls of the home, are largely responsible for the future social and public life of the country.

Just as we cannot take care of the child apart from the family, so his welfare is bound up with a lot of other institutions that influence his development – the school, the church, the agencies that offer useful interests for leisure time. . . . And the money and hard work that go into these public and private enter-prises are, again, repaid many times.[1]

As a nation, how far have we strayed from this vision? Raising children and educating them takes courage, but there are tremendous rewards. Parents and teachers can leave a legacy that will not be forgotten. But it can't stop there. We need to speak out beyond the walls of the home or classroom.

On behalf of all children, we need to turn our national priorities upside down, with spending for children at the top, and guns and bombs at the bottom – if we leave them there at all. New schools, not new prisons, could multiply across the country, and politicians could win on the most creative platform for education, not the toughest approach to crime or the most belligerent foreign policy.

The world needs children, but they also need us. We owe them more than mere survival. In the words of Indian poet Rabindranath Tagore:

> Children are living beings – more living than adults, who have built shells of habit around themselves. Therefore it is absolutely necessary for their mental health and development that they should have not only schools for their lessons, but a world whose guiding spirit is personal love.[2]

New children are born into our world every day, and as Tagore writes, each one brings "the renewed message that God has not lost faith in humankind." It is a mystical thought, but it carries a challenge as well. If the Creator has not lost hope in our humanity, who are we to do so?

Chapter 2

Play Is a Child's Work

Play is the highest expression of
human development in childhood,
for it alone is the free expression
of what is in a child's soul.

FRIEDRICH FROEBEL

True education can never be forced – a
child has to want to learn. This longing is often
locked deep inside, and it is the teacher's task to
discover and encourage it. But teaching has probably
never been as difficult as it is now. Many children
spend more hours each day with their caregivers than
with their parents. Too frequently, they come from
broken homes into understaffed and underfunded
classrooms. These children often enter the room
rebellious and guarded, blocking teachers out for fear
of being betrayed by yet another figure of authority.

But the role of the teacher is now more important than ever, and the most vital part of the work is not academic. We need to allow children to be children for as long as possible. They need time to breathe in and breathe out. They need to play. Children are not computers or robots that can be programmed according to our wishes; they have a heart and soul, not only a brain.

Friedrich Froebel, who created the concept of the kindergarten, was a nineteenth-century German educator whose greatest gift was his ability to view life through a child's eyes. That is why, almost two hundred years later, his educational philosophy makes sense to anyone who loves children. When he coined the name "kindergarten," he meant it literally – "a garden of children" – where each child is nurtured with the same love and care given to a seedling. He knew that humans are essentially creative and compassionate beings, and that education must involve the development of these traits.

Froebel often spoke of the importance of children's play: "A child who plays thoroughly and perseveringly, until physical fatigue forbids, will be a determined adult, capable of self-sacrifice both for his own welfare and that of others."

I have heard this quote all my life, as my mother, Annemarie, was Froebel's great-great-grandniece. My parents often spoke about his insights into childhood. As a matter of fact, Froebel's school in the little German village of Keilhau was run by my mother's family for many years, until the Nazis commandeered it.

My mother kept the vision of Keilhau alive through the war years, as her family migrated from Germany to England, then to Paraguay, and eventually to the United States. Because of her commitment to her educational heritage, my own children and grandchildren and many others have benefited from Froebel's approach. And we have seen that it works.

In *Froebel's Educational Laws for All Teachers,* educator James Hughes distills much of the wisdom of Keilhau into thoughts that are easily understood today:

> Froebel objected to every system that magnified knowledge at the expense of the child, and his whole life was a protest against the "stamping and molding" processes of teachers who failed to recognize the sacredness of the child's individuality. What he valued was not power, but creative power. He aimed to make something better of his pupils than mere "machines,"

and, as he so well said, to make them "free, thinking, independent people."[1]

Some of the greatest educational visionaries in America studied and built on Froebel's philosophy. Elizabeth Peabody was instrumental in the establishment of kindergartens across America. Caroline Pratt invented the concept of the unit block in 1913 and started City and Country School the next year. Lucy Sprague Mitchell founded the Bank Street College of Education with its focus on the early years. These women blazed the trail for learning through play, and their schools still stand as beacons for the education of the "whole child," emphasizing physical activity and creative expression.

Today advocates of play and exploration can be found everywhere. In fact, all good teachers know that play for its own sake is irreplaceable in a child's life. Not only is it the best method of early education, but it's also essential for the growth of a child's spirit. In a way, play ought to require no further defense; it defines childhood.

Yet in their document *Crisis in the Kindergarten,* Alliance for Childhood's Edward Miller and Joan Almon report that play continues to vanish from young children's lives. They back up their claim with studies and compelling evidence, and sum up their findings:

> Kindergarten has changed radically in the last two decades in ways that few Americans are aware of. Children now spend far more time being taught and tested on literacy and math skills than they do learning through play and exploration, exercising their bodies, and using their imaginations. Many kindergartens use highly prescriptive curricula geared to new state standards and linked to standardized tests. In an increasing number of kindergartens, teachers must follow scripts from which they may not deviate. These practices, which are not well grounded in research, violate long-established principles of child development and good teaching. It is increasingly clear that they are compromising both children's health and their long-term prospects for success in school.[2]

Some of the worst changes have originated from government-mandated academic programs that rob children of their chance to learn through play and burden teachers with ever more pressure and paperwork. As I watch this trend grow every year, I agree with Albert Einstein's observation: "It is a miracle that curiosity survives formal education."

The motives behind standardization often sound right. Politicians say they want to "fix" our broken educational system so our children can compete on the global stage. They talk about going back to basics, mastering the three Rs, and documenting measurable results. And many of these mandates are a direct result of parents and voters calling for change.

But we should look more closely at the kind of change that children need. Programs handed down from distant political establishments come with strings attached. Additional paperwork removes teachers from the children who need their care. Children are bewildered by tests and diagnostics at an age when they should be playing. Decision-makers, it seems, ignore the wisdom of the teachers who could – and do – tell them how children learn.

An example of this is a recent resignation letter from teacher Susan Sluyter, published in *The Washington Post:*

> I am writing today to let you know that I am resigning my position as Pre-K and Kindergarten teacher in the Cambridge Public Schools. It is with deep sadness that I have reached this decision, as I have loved my job, my school community, and the families and amazing and dedicated faculty I have

been connected with throughout the district for the past eighteen years.

In this disturbing era of testing and data collection in the public schools, I have seen my career transformed into a job that no longer fits my understanding of how children learn and what a teacher ought to do in the classroom to build a healthy, safe, developmentally appropriate environment for learning for each of our children.

I have experienced, over the past few years, the same mandates that all teachers in the district have experienced. I have watched as my job requirements swung away from a focus on the children, their individual learning styles, emotional needs, and their individual families, interests, and strengths to a focus on testing, assessing, and scoring young children, thereby ramping up the academic demands and pressures on them. Each year, I have been required to spend more time attending classes and workshops to learn about new academic demands that smack of first and second grade, instead of Kindergarten and Pre-K.

I have needed to schedule and attend more and more meetings about increasingly extreme behaviors and emotional needs of children in my classroom; I recognize many of these behaviors as children shouting out to the adults in their world, "I can't do

this! Look at me! Know me! Help me! See me!" I
have changed my practice over the years to allow the
necessary time and focus for all the demands coming
down from above. Each year there are more. Each
year I have had less and less time to teach the children
I love in the way I know best – and in the way child
development experts recommend. I reached the place
last year where I began to feel I was part of a broken
system that was causing damage to those very children I was there to serve.

I was trying to survive in a community of
colleagues who were struggling to do the same: to
adapt and survive, to continue to hold onto what we
could, and to affirm what we believe to be quality
teaching for an early childhood classroom. I began to
feel a deep sense of loss of integrity. I felt my spirit,
my passion as a teacher, slip away. I felt anger rise
inside me. I felt I needed to survive by looking elsewhere and leaving the community I love so dearly. I
did not feel I was leaving my job. I felt then and feel
now that my job left me.[3]

Many other teachers feel the same. But public policy
is against them, and they feel forced out of their field.
Teaching requires great love, wisdom, and patience.
It takes time to discover the best in each child, and
then to draw it out. What happens when teachers are

robbed of this precious time? When will they get the chance to build a relationship with each child through simple interaction and play, which is when the best teaching moments actually occur?

In Australia, educator Maggie Dent speaks out boldly in defense of play:

> Unstructured, child-centered play has enormous benefits for young children, and those benefits cannot be tested by benchmark testing. Our capacity to be creative thinkers and innovative problem-solvers comes from using our own mental processing to explore the world. How much do we need to value creative thinking, given the speed of change sweeping our modern world? There are no answers in text-books about how to manage unexpected change, and this is why we are disabling our children by stealing their capacity to use play to learn, to explore, to question, and to solve problems without an adult's assistance. They are biologically wired to learn from their experiences, provided those experiences are engaging and interesting.[4]

Every year children are further pressured to do "too much, too soon." But it's inspiring to hear stories of educators who bend or even break the rules for the sake of children. Dr. Sherone Smith-Sanchez, an educational administrator in New York City, shares her story:

> My husband and I flatly refused to let our son sit for the New York State tests. We chose to opt out when he was in third grade, and again this year for fourth grade. As educators, we're convinced that he is too young to understand the concept of testing for what a child doesn't know at the beginning of the year, then testing at the end to verify what he has or has not managed to memorize.
>
> Testing at such a young age does not synchronize with our aims for our son to become a critical thinker and a life-long learner. We know that children learn by association and hands-on action. We also know that if the pinnacle of his third or fourth grade educational experience is a test, then our son will go through anxiety whenever he's expected to share his knowledge in the future. We decided not to support this injustice to his age. We have shared our simple protest with others, and continue to encourage other parents and educators to speak up.

Madeleine, a mom from suburban Connecticut, tells of her search for a child-friendly alternative:

> In the end, several of us young families banded together to create our own kindergarten, so we

could postpone academics, at least until first grade, spending lots of time outdoors "learning with our hands." The best part of our little school is its location in a senior care center, where our children interact daily with the elderly, hearing their fascinating stories, becoming reading and lunch buddies, playing bat-the-balloon with the residents in the Alzheimer's wing.

Instead of learning their ABCs by memorizing a wall chart, they learn it by playing bingo with eighty-year-olds. They may not yet be as advanced in their studies as their public school counterparts, but we parents are not worried. The kids are bubbling with curiosity, excited to soak up new ideas, and ready to pick up "reading, writing, and arithmetic" as they apply to the experience at hand.

I watch my five-year-old daughter having a conversation with a grandmother who can now only speak with her eyes and her smiles. She's bent and wrinkled, she needs a wheelchair, and she's as full of life as the preschooler at her elbow. Across the room, there's the grandpa who says anything that comes into his head. Not once have I heard a sentence that I can put into any context of sense. The little boy who's chatting with him obviously has no such hang-up. They have been talking for ten minutes.

These children have been given a great gift. No longer afraid of age and disability, they receive as much as they give through these intergenerational interactions – and, without knowing it, are helping to mend the torn social fabric. For millennia, children have sat at the feet of the village elders to learn about life. Then, they would run off and play with whatever they could find to interest them. That, too, is learning.

In Finland and several other European countries, children only start academic instruction at age seven. These students have the lowest number of classroom hours in the developed world, yet they consistently score at the top of world education rankings by the end of their public school years. In these countries, it is simply understood that until age seven, children learn best when they're playing; by the time they finally get to school, they are eager to learn in a more formal setting. There is also greater public respect for teachers than in the United States, and correspondingly higher pay.[5]

There is profound truth in Plato's thought: "What is honored in a country is cultivated there." What is really honored in our country? Is it the forming of children's hearts and minds? Or is it career readiness?

In *The Education of Man,* Froebel writes:

> Protect the new generation; do not let them grow
> up into emptiness and nothingness, to the avoidance
> of good hard work, to introspection and analysis
> without deeds, or to mechanical actions without
> thought and consideration. Guide them away from
> the harmful chase after outer things and the damaging
> passion for distraction. . . . I would educate human
> beings who stand with their feet rooted in God's
> earth, whose heads reach even into heaven and there
> behold truth, in whose hearts are united both earth
> and heaven.[6]

Every child is different. Each has a unique set of
abilities, created for a special purpose. So why force
a common educational standard on them? We know
children learn best through playing, but play also
brings joy, contentment, and detachment from the
troubles of the day. In our frantically over-scheduled
culture, every child should have a right to play.

Chapter 3

Great Expectations

*I have always been regretting that I was
not as wise as the day I was born.*

HENRY DAVID THOREAU

In a magazine piece I read about a
Kenyan school that holds its classes in a shady
grove outdoors, the headmaster, who had helped
plant the trees as a child, recalled an African saying:
"When you plant a tree, never plant only one. Plant
three – one for shade, one for fruit, and one for
beauty." On a continent where heat and drought
make every tree valuable, that's wise advice.

It's also an intriguing educational insight for a time
like ours, when vast numbers of children are endangered by a one-sided parental approach that sees them
solely in terms of their ability to be fruitful – that is, to
"achieve" and "succeed." This pressure is destroying

childhood as never before. Child therapist Katie
Hurley writes:

> Academic pressure is only one piece of the puzzle
> when it comes to fast-tracking childhood. Yes,
> learning is accelerated across the board, but so is
> childhood in general. We've experienced a gradual
> cultural shift in this country, and it's becoming more
> and more prevalent with each passing year.
>
> It's true that young children are more likely to face
> intense academic pressure right now, but they are
> also overloaded with extracurricular activities. They
> play competitive sports (sometimes two sports during
> each "season"), they take the best music and art classes
> available, they join community-based programs and
> they fill their weekends with play dates and parties.
>
> Children are losing childhood because they aren't
> given the gift of time to play. That cultural shift – the
> intense need to raise competent, successful people –
> don't we all bear some responsibility for it? As a
> country, we need to wake up to the increased stress
> levels among children and learn how to dial it back.
> If we want to raise happy kids, we need to start by
> taking back childhood.[1]

Naturally, parents have always wanted their children
to do well, both academically and socially. No one
wants their child to be the slowest in the class, the

last to be picked for a game on the field. But what is it about the culture we live in that has made that natural worry into such an obsessive fear, and what is it doing to our children? For many, the trend toward fast-track academics makes school a place that they dread, a source of misery they cannot escape for months at a time.

Even though my grades were rarely exceptional, my parents cared far more about whether I got along with my peers than whether I achieved an A or a B. They assured me, especially when I didn't do well, that there was a lot more in my head than I or my teachers realized; it just hadn't come to the surface yet. Such encouragement is only a dream for many children, especially in homes where academic failure is seen as unacceptable.

My mother used to say that education begins in the cradle, and few parents today would disagree. But the differences in their approach are instructive. Whereas women of her generation sang their babies to sleep just as their mothers had done – because babies love the sound of their mother's voice – today's parents tend to cite studies on the positive effects of Mozart on the development of the baby's brain. Fifty years ago, women taught their toddlers finger games as a matter of course, purely for the sake of a good time spent together. How often do we set aside time for nursery rhymes now, despite endless discussion about the importance of bonding and nurture?

Mothers can and should be the best defenders of the sacredness of childhood. As the Spanish proverb goes, "An ounce of mother is worth a ton of priest." But parents today hear a louder message, telling them they must constantly crack the whip in order to keep their children ahead of the curve. Something is wrong with a culture when it informs a mother that her children's success rests on her ability to push them, or when it tells a father that good grades are the only measurement that matters.

To me, it's frightening that so many families have fallen into this trap. Now the results are beginning to trickle in, from teenagers and young adults who barely survived the strain and pressure, who missed the formative years of just being a child, and who never found that beautiful child-to-parent relationship of trust, acceptance, and encouragement. Novelist Kim Wong Keltner recalls her childhood:

All this chasing of straight As, this pushing, pushing, pushing for academic excellence, makes kids start to think their parents only care about who they are on paper. And ultimately, they may just decide: "If nothing is ever going to please you, why should I even try?". . .

I got good grades just to get my parents off my back. I got top test scores, but I was never encouraged to make connections with other people. And I never felt like I could separate myself from my parents; they would always say, "You're a part of me, what *you* do reflects on *me*."[2]

True, some survivors of this approach admit that without this parental drive, they wouldn't have such a successful career or make as much money as they do now. But what is the true meaning of success? What experiences in humanity and interaction were missed? We have to consider the next generation of children, and what they will learn from parents who never had a childhood.

Still, there are many parents who think deeply about what they want for their children, and who are inspired to change their emphasis. In an interview, author Paul Tough talks about what he wants his son to learn:

When Ellington was born, I was very much caught up in the idea of childhood as a race – the faster a child develops skills, the better he does on tests, the better he'll do in life. . . . [Now] I'm less concerned about my son's reading and counting ability. Don't get me wrong, I still want him to know that stuff. But I think he'll get there in time.

What I'm more concerned about is his character. . . . I want him to be able to get over disappointments, to calm himself down, to keep working at a puzzle even when it's frustrating, to be good at sharing, to feel loved and confident and full of a sense of belonging. Most important, I want him to be able to deal with failure.

That's a difficult thing for parents to give their children, since we have deep in our DNA the urge to shield our kids from every kind of trouble. But what we're finding out now is that in trying to protect our children, we may actually be harming them. By not giving them the chance to learn to manage adversity, to cope with failure, we produce kids who have real problems when they grow up. Overcoming adversity is what produces character.[3]

Children need a chance to learn that failure often teaches us more than success. Everyone goes through hard times, and these can be crucial for the development of a child's moral character. How else will they learn that the greatest triumph is the one that follows a defeat?

In his classic *Basics of Education,* German educator

Friedrich Wilhelm Foerster argues that the comforts of contemporary civilization have cushioned life so completely that many people grow up without the capability to deal with anything that makes demands on them. Faced with the simple unpredictability of life – not to mention pain, suffering, hard work, or sacrifice – they helplessly succumb, Foerster writes, "as if to hard blows. . . . They do not know what to make of frustration – how to make something constructive of it – and see it only as something that oppresses and irritates. And though these very things provided earlier generations with the experiences through which they gained mastery over life's challenges, they are often enough to send the rootless modern person into a mental institution."[4]

The tendency of parents to hover over their children, trying to eliminate all danger, risk, and frustration from life, can be damaging. In an article titled "Why Parents Need to Let Their Children Fail," teacher Jessica Lahey writes:

> I have worked with quite a number of parents who are so overprotective of their children that the children do not learn to take responsibility (and the natural consequences) of their actions. The children may develop a sense of entitlement and the parents

then find it difficult to work with the school in a trusting, cooperative, and solution-focused manner, which would benefit both child and school.

These are the parents who worry me the most – parents who won't let their child learn. You see, teachers don't just teach reading, writing, and arithmetic. We teach responsibility, organization, manners, restraint, and foresight. These skills may not get assessed on standardized testing, but as children plot their journey into adulthood, they are, by far, the most important life skills I teach.[5]

There are wonderful things to be learned from trying, failing, and trying again. If a project is not up to standard, a good teacher can help a child think about improvement and inspire him to do better. But that lesson is lost if the parent has completed the project for the child. And what message does that communicate? At some point, the child will need to face a challenge without a parent at his side. Will he look around for someone to take over, or will he step up? If his parents praise his half-hearted efforts so as not to threaten his "self-esteem," will he ever know the satisfaction of a difficult job well done?

This is where active and involved fathers can help.

I still maintain that no one has as much influence for good in a child's life as a mother. But a father's role is different and just as important, as Naomi Schaefer Riley, columnist and mother of three, points out:

> Dads are more likely to let their children take risks. It's not just that they'll actually let go when teaching kids how to ride a two-wheeler (something that I instinctively did not want to do when my kids were learning). . . .
>
> As psychologist Daniel Paquette has observed, "Fathers tend to stand behind their children so the children face their social environment, whereas mothers tend to position themselves in front of their children, seeking to establish visual contact."
>
> For years, we've known about the most basic effects of having a father's presence in the home: boys are less likely to commit crimes; girls are less likely to be taken advantage of by predatory men. But it turns out that dads may actually be doing a lot more: they're actually preparing our kids for modern life.
>
> By letting children engage in "unstructured play," by helping them gain the "grit" that comes with taking risks and letting them succeed or fail on their own, by pushing them to be a little more independent, it seems as though fathers may be the key to helping our children become, well, grown-ups.[6]

When I think about my own happy childhood, full of exploration and adventure, I wonder how we can help the children of today find confidence and daring. While I know there are dangers from which we must protect our children, it is easy to go too far down this road, with the result that children become timid and nervous.

Nature should not be a great, fearful unknown, to us or to our children. Let's make time to go exploring together. Whether it's the city park or neighboring woodland, this is where true learning and confidence-building happens. As famed naturalist Rachel Carson wrote, "If a child is to keep alive his inborn sense of wonder, he needs the companionship of at least one adult who can share it, rediscovering with him the joy, excitement, and mystery of the world we live in."

Every child needs to discover the magic of making snow angels, splashing in puddles, or climbing trees. Parents need to slow down and savor the precious years with the children God has entrusted to them. The years do not come back. Before you know it, your children are adults. The relationship you share then depends on the quality of the time spent together in their earliest memories.

As a child of European refugees who fled to South America during the Second World War, I grew up in the backwoods of Paraguay. My parents raised all seven of us children on Froebel's educational principles, focusing on the importance of play, singing, and storytelling, with the outdoors as our best classroom.

We had no fancy playgrounds and nothing that could be classified as play equipment. What we did have was a big sand pile and a nearby river where we would entertain ourselves for hours. These places became like friends to us. Here our imaginations could run wild, and we built castles, houses, and any other structures we could dream up. Being mostly outdoors, we discovered insects, plants, and animals.

We were completely satisfied with our adventures, and did not wish for anything more. We had such a great time that often our parents and teachers had difficulty getting us back to do our farm chores, of which there were plenty. In today's modern age, the importance of the sand pile can be rediscovered. If it kept me happy, it can surely keep other children happy!

Someone once gave my family a small monkey for a pet. We named him Berto. He was very lively and affectionate. Berto became a part of our family and

would jump on our shoulders as we went on walks.
We loved him very much. He had, however, one very
bad habit, which our neighbor Martin did not appreciate. Berto always ate up all the tomatoes and other
garden plants which Martin planted and nurtured
with great care and effort. Although his children
also enjoyed the monkey, Martin complained to my
father, Heinrich, about Berto's garden thievery. My
father had to find a way to get rid of the monkey. One
day he asked me to help him return Berto to the wild.

That was a hard day, and we children cried, unable
to imagine our family without him. I bravely went
along with my father, taking Berto deep into the
jungle. When we thought we had walked far enough,
my father let him go, and Berto very happily climbed
the closest tree. Monkeys are incredibly smart. They
can mimic human behavior, such as waving with
their paws, laughing, and crying. So as we turned and
walked away, Berto waved goodbye to us. We sadly
returned to our house.

Upon our return, Berto was waiting for us at the
door. He was very happy to see us and he waved his
arms to welcome us. After we had released him, he
must have swung from tree to tree at great speed, to
get to our house before we returned. We children

laughed and cried for joy, but we also knew he couldn't stay.

After a few days we took Berto back into the jungle. This time we went much further and crossed a river before we released him. We knew that because monkeys cannot swim, this parting would be final, and it would be the last time I could carry him on my shoulder. His departure left a big hole in our family, but gave me a new understanding for the ways of animals, from mimicry to homing instinct, and for the ways of humans, as we learn to let go of something we love.

My father was my hero. Another colorful chapter in our family history says as much about his active love and participation in our lives as it does about our animal adventures. Once he gave my little sister Maria a beautiful black cat which she named Puss. That summer, a severe epidemic of rabies swept through the area, killing cows, horses, and many family pets. The outbreak got worse and worse, decimating our livestock, which was our main source of income. In an effort to stem the spread of the disease, the local government ordered that all family pets should be exterminated. The four of us children pleaded with our father to find a way to save Puss.

So he built a little cage behind our house, where the cat stayed night and day. Every morning and evening he let the cat out down a little ladder, so Puss could relieve himself and return. Puss soon figured out the daily routine and would patiently wait for my father to arrive. Our cat had to be in complete isolation for six weeks, just so we could be certain that he was not carrying rabies. During this time, we were strictly forbidden to touch him. Finally, with great rejoicing, we were able to release Puss from his time in solitary confinement, which had saved his life. He was the only local cat that survived. And my father, by responding to his children's compassion instead of taking the easiest route, gave us another life lesson in integrity.

Looking back on my childhood, I realize that poverty and disease were rampant, and hard physical work was part of daily life. There was no indoor plumbing, no central heating, and, for many years, no electricity. Meals were cooked on an open fire, and there was always wood to split and stack, and water to carry. Grass was cut with a machete; it was coarse, heavy, and high, especially after rainfall. As a teenager, I grumbled about the never-ending chores, but my parents had no pity. And in retrospect I am grateful. I see now how their insistence taught me self-discipline, concentration, perseverance, and the ability to carry through – all things you need to be a father.

It's important to give children chores and expect them to contribute to the family on a daily basis. That is not the same as scheduling a continuous round of organized sports, clubs, and academics and robbing them of the time they need to develop on their own.

Granted, children ought to be stretched and intellectually stimulated. They should be taught to articulate their feelings, to write, to read, to develop and defend an idea, to think critically. But what is the purpose of the best academic education if it fails to prepare children for life?

The parental desire to have brilliant children is surely just another sign of our distorted vision – a reflection of the way we tend to view children as little adults. And the best antidote to that is to drop all of our adult expectations entirely, to get down on the same level as our children, to look them in the eye. Only then will we begin to hear what they are saying, to find out what they are thinking, and to see the goals we have set for them from their point of view. Only then will we be able to lay aside our own ambitions for them. As poet Jane Tyson Clement[7] writes:

Child, though I am meant to teach you much,
what is it, in the end,
except that together we are
meant to be children
of the same Father,
and I must unlearn
all the adult structure
and the cumbering years
and you must teach me
to look at the earth and the heaven
with your fresh wonder.

Chapter 4

Screening Out

It is not easy to straighten in the oak the crook that grew in the sapling.

GAELIC PROVERB

Children of the twenty-first century can navigate distant worlds from their video game controllers, but are not equipped with an understanding of the real world outside the window. Fascinating entertainment options have them hooked almost as soon as they can focus their eyes.

As parents and teachers, we know that too much technology is bad for children. And we've all heard horror stories about cyber-bullying, easily accessible porn sites, and online sexual predators. Parents can try to put controls on what their children can see and limit their access time. But what if the technology itself turns out to be bad for childhood?

In the United Kingdom, the *Telegraph's* education editor Graeme Paton calls attention to an alarming trend:

> Rising numbers of infants lack the motor skills needed to play with building blocks because of an "addiction" to tablet computers and smartphones, according to teachers. Many children aged just three or four can "swipe a screen" but have little or no dexterity in their fingers after spending hours glued to iPads. . . .
>
> Members of the Association of Teachers and Lecturers also warned how some older children were unable to complete traditional pen and paper exams because their memory had been eroded by overexposure to screen-based technology. They called on parents to crack down on tablet computer use and even turn off wi-fi at night to address the problem.[1]

Rhonda Gillespie is a baby and toddler specialist who has worked in early childhood education for decades. When I asked her what she thought about technology and children, she shared her own story:

> I have seen a devastating impact on children over the last twenty years. Technology attacks the foundation necessary for healthy development.

When I was a child, our neighborhood was safe and I played outside every day with my friends. We used our creativity and imagination, enhanced our problem solving skills and developed healthy bodies. But by the time my son was growing up, I rarely saw neighborhood children playing outside. The trend had shifted, and the outdoors was perceived to be unsafe.

I had to return to work full time, which meant long days and less evening time to play and enjoy the outdoors with my son. The biggest mistake I made was purchasing him his first video game console. It started off with rules and time limits, but as time progressed, so did the hours at the game controller.

At the beginning, it seemed like a win-win: he was interacting with children from all over the world and could casually socialize with his age group. He became good at some games and his confidence rose. I always thought that at some point he would find friends to play with in the neighborhood. Socialization has always been a challenge for him, and video game companies often bill their products as a bridge to forming connections. Now I feel he was denied the chance to develop healthy interactions.

My son is seventeen years old now. He will text all day long, but when he's around people, he does not know what to say or how to start a conversation.

He says he is comfortable talking to people on the computer because he does not get bullied. But the flip side is that he did not learn to work through those awkward childhood moments that are an opportunity for growth. If he had never had the choice of online "friends," would he have learned better social skills?

Part of childhood is about problem solving, working out strategies and solutions to everyday life issues. Life became easier with technology, but it also made children unfamiliar with the process of success: hard work and patience. We have created a generation that expects things immediately without effort. For example, when I was in school I would spend months on a research paper, taking many trips to the library, spending hours studying and collecting verified data. My son can now produce the same report in a few hours, on his computer, without the element of verification or proof.

The accessibility of screen devices has caused a significant decline in children's resilience, self-determination, desire for hard work, and sense of pride in achievement. And socialization among children is becoming extinct.

We know that physical health is affected by screen time – especially eyesight, hearing, and weight. But we also need to consider how it attacks a child's soul.

Many children find themselves unable to communicate with a real person who requires a thoughtful verbal response. More and more young children arrive at preschool with speech difficulties; some do not speak at all. Since this is a diagnosable trait in the autism spectrum, how many children may be categorized as autistic when they have simply not had the opportunity to learn human interaction?

In my conflict resolution work in schools, I sometimes speak with teens who don't know who they are – what is real about themselves and what is a mask. They have spent their growing years using several different personas or "avatars" in various imaginary worlds, and if they can make these false fronts more glamorous and bold than any mere human can hope to be, we should not be surprised that they come to hate themselves. This leads to desperation, depression, and in all too many cases, suicide.

On many levels, an addiction to video games is as dangerous as drug or alcohol abuse. It can lead children compulsively into ever darker worlds, with no easy way back. It's no surprise that so many school shootings have been carried out by avid gamers. They seem unable to differentiate between violent games and the consequences of murder in the real world, and incapable of feeling regret for their actions or compassion for their victims. We react with shock to hear about child soldiers commandeered into third-world armies. But it may be harder to see the young militias growing up in our own homes, manipulated just as cruelly as their more distant counterparts.

Now the first generation of gamers has come of parenting age, many without having overcome their addiction. Fathers come home from work only to disappear into a violent fantasy world. Games keep them trapped in adolescence; they spend hours in a parallel universe which absorbs the time that should be spent connecting with a child's reality – playing catch or reading a bedtime story.

Technology affects people of all ages, simply because it transfers our interest and consideration from human beings to machines. It's especially damaging for young children, who used to rely on the adults close to them for guidance and example. In his book, *Simplicity Parenting,* educator Kim John Payne touches on this point:

> The late MIT professor and pioneer of artificial intelligence Joseph Weizenbaum came to wonder about the appropriateness of computer technology for young children. He questioned whether we want to

expose our young children to artificial minds without human values or even common sense. Weizenbaum believed that there are transcendent qualities of human interaction that can never be duplicated by machines; he used as an example "the wordless glance that a father and mother share over the bed of their sleeping child."

Used too soon, does the two-dimensional screen of a computer actually interfere with a young child's complex learning systems of relationships and sensory exploration? I don't believe that computers should be a part of a young child's daily life. How curious will children be, how mentally agile, creative, and persistent in seeking answers to their questions, if, from a young age, they learn to Google first, and ask questions later (or not at all)?[2]

Even among the poorest families, it's rare to find a home without a television or computer. There may not be enough food in the cupboards, but television is considered mandatory. Though hardworking parents may point out that they can't afford a babysitter, and at least their children are home and safe, we need to ask, safe from what? Much of what is being absorbed can poison a child's spirit.

There is no easy way to relieve the burden that technology places on children. But if we love them, we can't slip into resignation just because we don't know where to start. One way to take action is to give children more "white space." In a book, white space is the room between the lines of type, the margins, the extra space at the beginning of a chapter. It allows the type to "breathe" and gives the eye a place to rest. White space is not something you're conscious of when you read a book. It is what isn't there. But if it were gone, you'd notice it right away. It is the key to a well-designed page.

Just as books require white space, so do children. They need room to grow, in a space shielded from the onslaught of the information age. It does not take a brilliant mind to see the effects of a lack of white space. When children are overwhelmed by entertainment, material goods, high pressure academics, and frequently unstable home life, it's as if their flashlight batteries are being run down. Their light gets dimmer, and they don't know what's wrong. If we deny them the time, space, and flexibility they need to develop at their own pace, they will not be able to recharge their batteries.

The ancient Chinese philosopher Lao-Tzu reminds us that "it is not the clay the potter throws that gives the jar its usefulness, but the space within."

If stimulation and guidance are the clay, then time
by oneself is the space within. Hours spent alone
in daydreams or in quiet, unstructured activities –
preferably out in nature – instill a sense of security
and independence and provide a necessary lull in
the rhythm of the day. Children thrive on silence.
Without external distractions they will often become
so inspired by what they are doing that they will
be totally oblivious of everything around them.
Unfortunately, silence is such a luxury that they are
rarely allowed the opportunity for such undisturbed
concentration.

As parents and caregivers, how can we find
creative ways to give children more silence and space?
In schools, some teachers stand at the classroom door
with a bag, confiscating all phones and tablets for
the duration of the class so that children can focus.
Others send home letters to parents requesting less
entertainment time after school hours. They point out
that children are more likely to get their homework
done and have a good night's sleep. They explain
that the less violence is absorbed, the less fighting,
arguing, and bullying happens in school.

I know of others who have negotiated with their
school administration to remove technology from

the classroom – an uphill battle now that computers have come to be considered indispensable. I think these teachers have a sound argument: since children spend so many hours at home glued to one screen or another, does it benefit their education or physical well-being if the school ensures they do the same during the day? If the result is restlessness, aggressive behavior, and lack of focus, does it advance the school's goals?

In Los Altos, California, children of Google, Apple, and Hewlett-Packard executives attend a Waldorf School. *The New York Times* reports:

> The school's chief teaching tools are anything but high-tech: pens and paper, knitting needles and, occasionally, mud. Not a computer to be found. No screens at all. They are not allowed in the classroom, and the school even frowns on their use at home.
>
> Schools nationwide have rushed to supply their classrooms with computers, and many policy makers say it is foolish to do otherwise. But the contrarian point of view can be found at the epicenter of the tech economy, where some parents and educators have a message: computers and schools don't mix. . . .
>
> Teacher Cathy Waheed, who is a former computer engineer, tries to make learning both irresistible and highly tactile. Last year she taught fractions by

having the children cut up food – apples, quesadillas, cake – into quarters, halves and sixteenths. "For three weeks, we ate our way through fractions," she said. "When I made enough fractional pieces of cake to feed everyone, do you think I had their attention?" . . .

"Teaching is a human experience," says Paul Thomas, a former teacher and an associate professor of education at Furman University. "Technology is a distraction when we need literacy, numeracy, and critical thinking." . . .

And where advocates for stocking classrooms with technology say children need computer time to compete in the modern world, Waldorf parents counter: what's the rush, given how easy it is to pick up those skills?[3]

If executives in the world of high technology choose a school that protects their children from computers, other parents and teachers need to hear about it. But even if schools are unwilling to scrap their venerated technology, there are outdoor programs which can do wonders for a child's confidence. Sometimes, all children need is a chance to find out for themselves that the real world is more interesting than the virtual world. Laurie Rankin, who works with the "Big Brothers Big Sisters" program, tells this story:

I was leading a hike in the Catskills – we had great weather and a good turnout. I particularly remember Lance, age thirteen, who arrived with his headphones on, playing loud music and informing me belligerently, "I don't want to be here." I said, "Thank you for joining us!" His younger sister Jess, eleven, was quiet and shy. As we passed large boulders along the forest trail, I suggested she might like to try rock climbing. Shyly, she answered, "No, I can't do that." I continued to encourage her and finally, with my assistance, she climbed very carefully to the top of a rock. She almost stood up, but then, frightened, came right back down, with a big smile on her face.

I noticed Lance was watching. We stopped at the next rock and this time Jess climbed to the top and triumphantly raised her arms above her head. Lance slid the headphones down around his neck and suggested that she should be careful. But at the next rock pile, Lance was climbing with his sister, suggesting hand holds and foot placements and joining the triumph on top.

To see this sibling team gain confidence that day was magnificent. The tensions they may feel at other junctures in their lives – such as having to read a passage aloud in class, or discussing a wrongdoing with an adult – will be made lighter because they conquered some rocks.

The following year, the first person out of the van was Lance. There were no headphones in sight. He couldn't wait to show me what he had in his back-pack: some gloves for the kids to wear when rock climbing and some rope in case they were scared. The belligerent boy from last year was replaced by a young man who was a leader in the group.

We don't all live as close to forests and streams as we might wish. But creative teachers can do a lot with a little. Dana Wiser, a friend of mine, remembers how his daughter's teacher found a way to give her students white space during the day:

> When my daughter Mary was in first grade, she was lucky to have a teacher wise in the ways of both children and nature. She encouraged every child to adopt one of the trees that were grouped around the children's playground. Mary's "pet tree" was a sycamore, strong and tall, and of a girth she could hide behind. Each child studied the adopted tree, tracing its leaves and bark pattern. Quiet time spent with their pet trees was extra special, and when something about the school day upset Mary, all she had to do was visit her sycamore, drawing solace from its strength and comfort from its shade. She will love all trees, and especially sycamores, all her life; more than that,

something of nature's healing power lives in her heart
as a gift from her pet tree.

White space and nature can be healing for troubled
children. But, like most remedies, they work better
if taken preventatively. We can proactively make
changes before things get desperate. Can you do
without a television? Thousands of families do, with
heartening results. Having grown up without one,
I found it easier to leave it out of my own home,
sparing our children the advertising that would
relentlessly inform them, among other things, of
further advanced technology that they "just had
to have."

If several nearby families opt for freedom from
screens, it can become a groundswell movement.
Children can play together and adults won't feel as if
they're the only ones out of step with the times.

In my house, as in many, computers are merely
tools for adults to do their work; we don't turn to
them for entertainment. My kids only learned typing
in middle school, when their term papers were long
enough to warrant the effort. Parents can support
their children's research, teaming up for internet
searches if they're required, but also taking library
trips together and swapping books. It's a great

chance to point out that on the web, anyone can say anything, but that doesn't mean it's true.

World news should be a part of a child's education, but it does not need to be accompanied by graphic images. It is hard enough for us adults to process the pain and suffering we see in the news each day without becoming jaded or allowing it to harden our hearts. If adults take the time to read up on current events or listen to public radio, we can approach difficult subjects in a way that respects a child's age and understanding. This can provide an opening for further discussion about world suffering and what can be done to alleviate it.

The catch, of course, is our own time. In our over-scheduled adult lives, we're not sure we have time to work and play together with our kids, or sit and talk about the news. At school, the ominous curriculum deadlines can prevent teachers from taking their kids out to associate with trees.

But when we think of the alternatives, it is worth making time, and making it now. We only have these few years together. Society may lament an epidemic of lost, cynical teens, incapable of compassion or empathy. But if children's spirits aren't guided and protected by those closest to them, what do we expect?

It's time for us to take a hard look at all the clever devices in our own lives that everyone calls time-savers. When we sit texting on a playground bench while our kids play alone, whose time are we saving? When we send one more email, read one more article, play one more round of a video game while children are in the vicinity, we're telling them that something else is more important than they are. We can talk about children's technological addictions all we want, but the problem starts closer to home.

Let's put our smartphones away and tune in to the living, breathing wonders who are waiting for us to look up and notice them. Let's shut off the power, take our child by the hand, and show them that the real world is a fascinating place.

Chapter 5

Material Child

Where your treasure is,
there will your heart be also.

JESUS OF NAZARETH

In an age where the dollar has cast its spell
over every corner of public and private life, the most
insidious danger to children may be the economic lens
through which we view them. As would-be parents
debate the burden, risk, or liability of investing in children, other parties are calculating assets and benefits.

In other words, the same materialism that breeds
such hostility toward children also welcomes them
with open arms when they have money to spend.
Labor laws may have removed children from the
workforce in the western world, but our generation
has its own, equally effective form of enslavement:
the discovery of the child as a consumer. Not content
to pick the pockets of adults to fuel the economy,

advertisers have discovered the most lucrative market of all: children. The easiest targets and the most persuasive wheedlers, today's children and teens have been successfully harnessed to tug on their parents' heartstrings till they get what they want.

Corporations that set their sights on children before they have even learned to talk are engaging in nothing less than child abuse. Studies show that until they're eight, most children can't even differentiate between a sales pitch and a story.[1] Advertising divides us parents from our children. It gets there first, stealing our opportunities to be a gatekeeper and protector. Instead, we are playing catch-up, trying to un-teach something they heard from a convincing source. Parents who contradict the "buy-this-now" mantra find their children accusing them of meanness and misunderstanding. How many times have we heard, "everyone else has this" or "everyone else does that"?

Marketers have found hundreds of ways to disparage parents and exploit a child's natural tendency to rebel against the very people whose guidance they need most. But whose authority do they accept instead? Should a company tell your child who her friends should be, or how she should dress, speak, act, and think?

Unfortunately, schools can become conduits for companies as well. In districts around the country, financial incentives such as computers, online textbooks, sports equipment, and vending machines are being used to coax principals into signing deals with big name corporations who gain the exclusive right to market their wares to a captive young audience.

Despite the fact that millions around the globe grow up in acute poverty, most children in developed regions like western Europe and the United States have far more than they need. We are raising a generation of what can only be called spoiled brats. But let's not put all the blame on a steady diet of commercials. This problem has deeper roots.

Spoiled children are often the product of spoiled parents – parents who insist on getting their own way, and whose lives are structured around the illusion that instant gratification brings happiness. Children are spoiled not only by an overabundance of food, toys, clothing, and other material things. It's just as easy to spoil them simply by giving in to their whims. How many exhausted mothers spend all of their energy keeping up with their children's demands, giving in just to keep them quiet?

Clearly, it is one thing to cater to a child's wishes. To create a home – a place of love and security – is quite a different matter. Unfortunately, many parents today lack a sense of what this means. They are "too busy" to spend time with their children. Some are so preoccupied with their jobs or their leisure activities that even when they do see their children at the end of a long day, they have no energy to be with them. They may sit in the same room – even on the same couch – but their minds are elsewhere.

If we blame our children's selfishness on the media, we won't tackle the greed in our own hearts. Our children can see how much money and time we spend on ourselves. The best way to help them is to confront our own obsession with stuff and to turn outward, toward them and toward others.

In their book, *Making Grateful Kids,* Jeffrey J. Froh and Giacomo Bono point to a solution:

> If there were a new wonder drug on the market that got kids to behave better, improve their grades, feel happier, and avoid risky behaviors, many parents around the world would be willing to empty their bank accounts to acquire it. Amazingly, such a product actually does exist. It's not regulated by the FDA, it has no ill side effects, and it's absolutely free

and available to anyone at any time. This miracle cure
is gratitude.[2]

Isn't it strange that the more gifts a child receives,
the rarer it is to hear a thank-you? As parents and
teachers, we need to rediscover and guide our children
back to the concept of "less is more." This will take
creativity. I know one father who took time with his
six-year-old son, explaining that their family had fallen
for a sneaky trick from some companies who just
wanted to make money. He challenged his son to look
through his room and pull out all the things he had
gotten because of an advertisement. Then the dad went
to his den and did the same! The child ended up with
a bed, a chair, and a table. The dad ended up with an
empty room, and a lot more time with his son.

Another family pretended they were traveling to
California by Conestoga wagon, and had to get rid
of all the nonessentials. If parents and children unite
against the advertisements, the greatest battle has
already been won.

One of the best ways to foster gratefulness is to
connect with others who are not so materially blessed.
It's no use trying to get a child to appreciate his dinner
by generalizing: "Children in Africa are starving." I
doubt such a statement has ever convinced a picky

eater. But if a family or a school class becomes pen
pals with a child in Uganda, perhaps sponsoring her
schooling, suddenly it will make sense. Visualizing the
obstacles that some courageous children must overcome to eat one meal a day or to obtain an education
can leave an impression – and build a friendship – that
lasts for life.

There are other points of connection. Some families
have a "toy in, toy out" policy; if a new toy arrives,
another leaves the house and goes to someone who
needs it. But learning about gratefulness has to go
beyond toys and material goods. Volunteering at a
soup kitchen, especially on holidays like Thanks-
giving, can help children understand the meaning of
thankfulness.

Parents should not be afraid to do something
drastic. It's going to take a decision of some magni-
tude to counter the all-pervasive message of "look out
for number one." Our society has been steeped in it
for so long that flipping off a few switches here and
there will not be enough to reverse the trend or help
your child.

British mother Hattie Garlick documented her
family's experience after they decided not to spend any

money on children's products for a year. Six months into the experiment, she wrote:

> I began to see that a lack of self-confidence was behind a lot of my spending. My husband and I don't have any family within an hour's drive of our home. Without the advice and support of relatives to lean on, there were times when I felt scared, incompetent, and alone.
>
> I was easy prey for product marketers. I remember standing in the baby aisle of a department store jiggling a screaming, colicky infant, my eyes and mind blurred by a rainbow of pastel-colored goods promising to "soothe" and "comfort" my angry child, as I had failed to do. Exhausted, and desperate to do the right thing, I'd fallen for the idea that I wasn't enough on my own. To be a good parent, I needed all these props – educational mobiles that played Beethoven sonatas, baby sign language classes and purees put together in a factory. . . .
>
> There is a prevalent feeling among parents that, with expensive classes and entertainment all around us, simply leaving your child to play outside with a stick must count as lazy or, worse, uncaring. But over the months, we've found that most of the activities that we enjoy doing together are, in fact, free: cooking, gardening, foraging, even just getting together with

neighbors for coffee and "music lessons" (everyone brings whatever instruments they've got, or even just pots and pans, and we turn the music up loud). . . .

It turns out my son Johnny will happily spend hours building something out of a cardboard box, but only be amused by a new toy for a few minutes. We're tending to tadpoles and vegetables in the garden now, and Johnny takes it really seriously. He takes his grandparents out there when they come round, and they watch the birds and butterflies and talk about how plants grow.[3]

Children don't see material benefits in the same way adults do. From my childhood in South America, I recall a visitor who asked me and my sisters if it was hard to live so simply. Looking up at the stranger, I wondered if he was crazy. Hard? What on earth did he mean? I couldn't imagine a happier childhood. But now I understand the foundation of our happiness. Instead of things, my parents gave us time and attention on a daily basis. No matter how hectic their schedule, they tried to eat breakfast with us before we went off to school each morning.

The idea of gathering as a family, for a meal or simply to end the day together, has fallen by the wayside. Even if we wish for it, conflicting schedules and long commutes often make it impossible. But regardless of the reason, it is the children who lose out, and I am not convinced that it is always a matter of economic necessity.

Though my parents worked long hours, they made a point of drawing us all in at the end of the day to gather and regroup. Our generation needs to reclaim this concept of anchoring a family to give the children a foundation. It takes sacrifice on the part of both parents, but the results make it completely worthwhile.

I have been amazed to find, on my travels around the world, that in some of the most impoverished places on earth, in Africa, South America, and the Middle East, there is also the greatest devotion to family and children. These places lack all of the material advantages we take for granted in the developed sectors of the West. Infant mortality rates are high, water is polluted, food is meager, and medicines are always in short supply, if they are available at all. Toys are sticks or tin cans, clothes are ragged, babies lack cribs and strollers. Yet nowhere have I seen such radiant smiles, such warmhearted hugs, or such great affection between parents and teens, elderly people and small children.

What is it about the plush homes of our own country, where every material need is more than adequately attended to, that leaves our children in such a different state? Maybe it is the lack of something to live and work for beyond a better car and a bigger house.

I won't romanticize poverty. Nor am I blind to the fact that there are many poor children in the "developed world," from the migrant camps in Florida and California to the ghettos of New York and London's East End. In those places and others too numerous to name, children are being denied the most basic necessities – let alone the additional trappings that most of us feel we deserve. Deprivation gives rise to neglect and abuse. These children are in my prayers daily, and their suffering is a judgment on a society where many other children are suffocating in overabundance. I firmly believe that the well-being of a child is not dependent on his or her access to material wealth, but on the knowledge that he or she is loved.

Mother Teresa once observed, after a visit to North America, that she had never seen such an abundance of things. But, she went on, she had also never seen "such a poverty of the spirit, of loneliness, and of being unwanted. . . . That is the worst disease in the world today, not tuberculosis or leprosy. . . . It is the poverty born of a lack of love."

What does it mean to give a child love? Many parents, especially those whose work keeps them away from their families for days or even weeks at a time, try to overcome feelings of guilt by bringing home gifts. Well-meaning as they are, they forget that what their children really want, and need, is time and attentiveness, a listening ear, and an encouraging word.

Deep down, every parent knows that bringing up a child entails more than providing for them. It's a rare father or mother who won't readily admit that they ought to take more time with their children. My father often said that investing in time spent with your children is more important than investing in your bank account.

Obviously, it is impossible to live without money and material goods, and every household must have its provider and its plans for the future. But ultimately it is the love we give our children, and not the material things, that will remain with them for life. And that is something we all too easily forget with the lure of a bigger paycheck or a better job.

Dale, a good friend, used to work for one of the largest law firms in the world. Though he once made more money per year than many people make in a lifetime, his paycheck and his prestige meant little to his family – perhaps because he was never at home to enjoy it with them. Excuses didn't go over well, either with his wife or his children, so rather than dig in his heels, Dale decided to try listening. Soon he had heard enough and made up his mind that there was only one thing to do – quit the firm. As he tells it:

> A colleague and I were driving home from a Cub Scout gathering. While the van-full of boys played and laughed in the back seats, he cleared his throat and broached a difficult subject. "Dale, you are making a big mistake by leaving the law firm. Do you realize that?" He was referring to my decision to give six months' notice of my resignation. "It's not like you can just do whatever you want," he continued. "You have five children. You have a duty to give them the best life possible and to send them to the best universities they can get into. You are shirking your duty."
>
> I let a few moments pass. Finally, I replied. "It wasn't my idea. I never intended to cut back to less than twenty hours per week. My daughters pleaded that I quit."

It was true. For the last two years I had balanced twenty hours per week as a lawyer with an equal amount of time serving men dying of AIDS and cancer. This was a dramatic change from my life as a lawyer who lived on airplanes, opening accounts all over the country and working eighty to ninety hours a week. But when the Iraq war hit, my part-time legal work suddenly exploded, and soon I was back to my old schedule.

About six weeks into this reversion, my daughter disappeared from school: she simply wasn't there one afternoon when we went to pick her up. We looked for her for over two hours and finally contacted the police. Later she was found by a friend walking alone on a roadside, crying. Her explanation was simple: "Dad, when you were gone all the time, it didn't matter. But now I've gotten used to you being here, and I can't take it. I want you to quit being a lawyer."

First I tried to get my older daughter to talk some sense into her younger sister, but it didn't work. She agreed with her completely. Then I put it all down on paper for them to contemplate – to show them just how stiff the economic consequences would be: pay for your own clothes, car, gas, insurance, yearbooks, prom, college, trips, etc. It didn't matter. My daughters wanted me.

My colleague was bringing the van to a stop at a red light. "Look," he said impatiently. "You're avoiding your responsibility!" A few moments passed before I sealed the discussion. It seemed too important to finish quickly. I was focusing on a clump of trees that refused to fall in line, refused to be controlled, refused to be cut down and processed at the corporate mill.

"I disagree," I told him gently. "I disagree. And I bet, in your heart of hearts, that you do, too."

Chapter 6

Actions, Not Words

Don't worry that your children never listen to you. Worry that they are always watching you.

ROBERT FULGHUM

Most of us know what's good or bad for children. Unfortunately, there's a gulf between knowing what you want for a child, and being able to ensure that he or she acts accordingly. It's clear that in many homes the gulf is not being bridged.

When children and teens throw themselves into Goth culture, gangs, sexual relationships, or drugs, they're not blind to all risks. In most cases, parents and teachers have made numerous appeals on behalf of their future, their health, and their ability to contribute to society in a positive way. But children aren't dumb. If as far as they can tell, what their parents really care about is their grades, they rebel.

As conventional wisdom goes, teenage angst is "just a phase." Adolescents have always chafed under parental authority, and they always will. When rebellion becomes a way of life, however, we cannot brush it off. We need to look a little deeper. What is it that today's children are rebelling against so vigorously, and why?

To me, the answer is simple: hypocrisy. The word is admittedly a strong one; it may even seem cruel to suggest that there are parents who raise their children to act one way while simultaneously doing the opposite. But the hard truth is that this does happen – in far too many ways. Consider this anguished outpouring from a student at Texas A&M who felt compelled to explain, after a school massacre, why she thought things had "become so bad":

> Let me tell you this: these questions don't represent only me but a whole generation that is struggling to grow up and make sense of this world.
>
> Why did most of you lie when you made the vow of "'til death do us part"?
>
> Why do you fool yourselves into believing that divorce really is better for the kids in the long run?
>
> Why do you allow us to watch violent movies but expect us to maintain some type of childlike innocence?

Why do you allow us to spend unlimited amounts of time on the Internet but still are shocked about our knowledge of how to build bombs?

Why are you so afraid to tell us "no" sometimes?

Call us what you want to, but you will be surprised how we will fail to fit into your neat little category. . . . Now is the time to reap what you have sown.[1]

Accusing as these questions are, I believe every one of them is valid, and vital for us to consider. Many of the issues they raise are too complex to answer in a few words, but they all touch on one central issue: the widespread perception of young adults that their elders are frauds.

Hypocrisy rears its head early in parenting, but it mostly appears in very subtle ways. Sometimes it is rooted in the confusion that arises when a child hears one thing at school and another at home, one direction from one parent and a second from the other, one set of guidelines in one classroom, and an entirely different set in the next. In other instances, it stems from simple inconsistency: a child has just learned a lesson or a rule, only to find her parent breaking it, making an exception, or explaining it away. All this is usually harmless enough.

The real problem arises – and this is more wide-spread than one might think – when children are taught to "do as I say, not as I do." Told this half-jokingly in one situation after another, they gradually learn that there is never anything so black and white that it is always good or bad, at least not until they make the wrong choice at the wrong time. When that happens, they get punished for their lapse of judgment. And they will always find the punishment unjust.

Being a father, I know how hard it is to be consistent – and conversely, how easy it is to send confusing signals without even realizing it. Having counseled hundreds of teenagers over the last four decades, I also know how sensitive young adults are to mixed messages and inconsistent boundaries, and how readily they will reject both as clear signs of parental hypocrisy. But I have also learned how quickly the worst battle can be solved when we are humble enough to admit that our expectations were unclear or unfair, and how quickly most children will respond and forgive.

Reflecting on the ways in which children so often mirror their parents – in actions, attitudes, behavioral characteristics, and personal traits – my grandfather, writer Eberhard Arnold, noted that children are like barometers. They visibly record whatever influences and pressures currently affect them, whether positive or negative. Happiness and security, generosity and optimism will often show themselves in children to the same degree that they are visible in their parents. It is the same with negative emotions. When children notice anger, fear, insecurity, or intolerance in an adult – especially if they are the target – it may not be long before they are acting out the same things.

In *The Brothers Karamazov,* Dostoyevsky's character Father Zossima reminds us that this sensitivity of children is so great that we shape them without even knowing it, and he admonishes us to consider the effect of everything we say – and especially everything we do – in their presence:

> Every day and hour . . . see that your image is a seemly one. You pass by a little child, you pass by spiteful, with ugly words, with wrathful heart; you may not have noticed the child, but he has seen you, and your image, unseemly and ignoble, may remain in his defenseless heart. You don't know it, but you may have sown an evil seed in him, and it may grow . . . all because you did not foster in yourself an active, actively benevolent love.[2]

Unlike the children of Dostoyevsky's time, children today are exposed to a steady barrage of images and expressions whose combined effect may be far greater than that of the most caring adult in their immediate lives. Given the state of our culture, which undercuts parents at every turn, bringing up children is hard work. But despite all our efforts, most of us are far from the models we ought to be.

Take violence. Everyone is concerned about it, and everyone agrees it is bad for children. But what is anyone really doing about it? From the halls of Congress on down, precious little. Politicians bicker about gun control, but is decisive action ever taken? Meanwhile the spate of school shootings continues, spawning ever more imitators.

Several times I have had the privilege of counseling victims' families. Naturally, they needed time to talk and weep through their hurt and confusion, without having to cope with analysis and advice. But inevitably our conversation would come around to the root causes of school violence. Writing about this, novelist Barbara Kingsolver points out the contradictions in our attempts to address violence:

> Let's not trivialize a horrible tragedy by pretending we can't make sense of it. "Senseless" sounds like

"without cause," and requires no action. After an appropriate interval of dismayed hand-wringing, we can go back to business as usual. What takes guts is to own up: this event made perfect sense.

Children model the behavior of adults, on whatever scale is available to them. Ours are growing up in a nation whose most important, influential men – from presidents to film heroes – solve problems by killing people. It's utterly predictable that some boys who are desperate for admiration and influence will reach for guns and bombs. And it's not surprising that it happened in a middle-class neighborhood; institutional violence is right at home in the suburbs. Don't point too hard at the gangsta rap in your brother's house until you've examined the Pentagon in your own. [These tragedies] grew straight out of a culture that is loudly and proudly rooting for the global shootout. That culture is us.

It may be perfectly clear to you that Nazis, the Marines, and the Terminator kill for different reasons. But as every parent knows, children are good at ignoring or seeing straight through subtleties we spin.

Here's what they see: killing is an exalted tool for punishment and control. Americans who won't support it are ridiculed. Let's face it, though, most Americans believe bloodshed is necessary for preserving our way of life, even though this means we risk the occasional misfire – the civilians strafed, the innocent man wrongly condemned to death row.

... In a society that embraces violence, this is what "our way of life" has come to mean. We have taught our children in a thousand ways, sometimes with flag-waving and sometimes with a laugh track, that the bad guy deserves to die.[3]

Clearly, the way we deal with violence is not just a social or political phenomenon, but something that has roots in every living room. Children see it on screen, or experience it at the hands of those who should be their protectors. But the issue here isn't just violence. No matter the vice or virtue, it is utterly futile to try to educate a child about it as long as our deeds and words remain at odds with each other. As psychologist Carl Jung states, "If there is anything we wish to change in the child, we should first examine it and see whether it is not something that could be better changed in ourselves."

Often the root cause of the divide between our words and actions is simply laziness. This may be a harsh word, and none of us would like to apply it to ourselves. But we should ask ourselves: When confronted with a crisis in the life of one of our children, do we take the easy way out, responding with annoyance, or perhaps a swift consequence, and then forgetting about it till the next time it happens?

Perhaps we're busy, overwhelmed, or simply tired. But children can sense dishonesty in this automatic response. If a son or daughter tests our limits, he or she may be trying to find a secure boundary to lean against. Though the tendency to settle for the most painless solution to a problem is a normal human trait, it is rarely a healthy approach to child rearing.

The very idea that parenting is a "problem" is negative. After all, raising the children we bring into the world ought to be a privilege. Yet fewer and fewer parents view our inherent responsibilities in positive terms. As a result, fatherhood is no longer a natural duty, but an obligation the government must compel men to fulfill; motherhood is at once attacked and seen as the supreme sacrifice; and loving your child is regarded as an art or a skill that requires special training.

From parenting journals to popular books, the wisdom is the same: children may be cute, but raising them is a thankless chore. That's why magazines are always advising couples to get away for romantic candlelight dinners, for vacations or long weekends by themselves. Just don't ask where the children fit into these plans: they rarely do – which is sad, because in actual fact, it's the hours you spend with your children when they are growing up that can later stand out as some of the happiest of your marriage. As for the struggles, sacrifices, and hard times, they are just as formative. Happy memories are just that – happy – but it's the rough patches that really strengthen relationships.

Why do we try to dodge the hard parts of parenting, blind to the ways they could help us to grow? Clare, a member of my church, says:

> Perhaps it's because our generation never really grew up. Many of us are still seeking the perfect partner, the perfect car, or some other kind of elusive happiness. We don't know what it is to make sacrifices, to give unselfishly in ways that won't ever be recognized. I'm not sure we were ever expected to.

Sometimes we skirt a difficult issue simply because we feel too weary to confront it. At other times our reluctance is connected to guilt: Why be hard on our children when we've made the same mistakes? Or how can we give them clear advice when our own lives and relationships are murky? Such thinking rarely has immediate consequences, but it will eventually catch up with us. Bea, an acquaintance, gives a poignant example:

I had a friend, Kate, who tried to commit suicide three times in high school. Her family always rushed her to the emergency room, and had her stomach pumped (she took pills each time), and she'd soon be back at school. They never really helped her. . . . Kate's parents had divorced some years before, and then remarried, and neither set of parents really wanted her. She was a constant reminder to them of their pasts, and they wanted to get on with their lives. She didn't fit into their plans.

How many children do not fit into the plans of the people who gave them life? More to the point, how often do we put ourselves and our desire for "happiness" and "fulfillment" above the needs of our children?

Sex is another sphere where even the most well-meaning parents confuse children – if not with hypocrisy, then at least with conflicting messages. Like violence, sex is one of every parent's biggest concerns, and one of the most talked about. But amid all the worry about what to say to our sons and daughters, how to say it, and when, many of us are forgetting the most important thing: the power of our actions. Until we start living our convictions – until we demand of ourselves the same things we demand of our children – all our strenuous efforts at modeling integrity will fall flat.

What passes for family structure today may satisfy the adults in the relationship (at least for a time). If they have never witnessed a faithful, stable marriage, parents may have no basis on which to form their own commitments, and they may not be aware of the enormous impact their drifting will have on their children, who crave stability.

Statistically, separation and divorce have long been likely outcomes of marriage. But they are never the one-time legal incidents they appear. That is why – no matter how "necessary" the divorce may seem – we need to look at it through the eyes of the child who may be defined by it, emotionally and psychologi-cally, for the rest of her life.

Still, it is heartless to condemn couples who divorce. As Anne, an English friend whose father left when she was a child, says, "Adults in crisis are desperate, and do what they must." Though Anne concedes that children usually bear the brunt of the consequences, she notes that adults pay too. And she reminds us that the pain caused by divorce need not be the end of the story:

I had a very good mother, and even after she made the choice for divorce (the only option she saw), she was faithful to me. She sacrificed the joys of motherhood and worked full-time to support me, and her loyalty pulled me through. She gave me her best years – twenty-one of them.

Yes, divorce always scars both partners, and if they have children, it scars them even more. But from my own life, I know that my mother's decision to put my needs before hers saved me. It offered me the chance of recovery. I'm still "on the road," but I know full healing and wholeness will come.

Without the resilience shown by every child who overcomes the obstacles of adult hypocrisy and failings, parenting would indeed be a bleak challenge. Stories like Anne's show us that no matter how tempting it may be to despair over past mistakes, even the worst father or mother has a right to hope.

Addressing the question of parental shortcomings, and reminding us of the source of that hope, Malcolm X once wrote:

Children teach us a lesson adults should learn: to not be ashamed of failing, but to get up and try again. Most of us adults are so afraid, so cautious, so "safe" and therefore so shrinking and rigid. . . . That is why so many humans fail. Most middle-aged adults have resigned themselves to failure.[4]

While my plea for honesty and action in this chapter is addressed primarily to parents, by no means do these issues end when a child climbs onto the school bus. In fact, as many teachers have experienced, home life, whether stable or shaky, makes its presence felt in every child and every classroom. Often, when anger and rebellion are hurled at us as teachers, we need to remind ourselves that we're the lightning rod, not the target. It takes enormous patience to love a child who has lost his bearings due to circumstances beyond our reach.

Sandy Miller is one educator who has made a profound difference in many children's lives. I have known and worked with her for almost three decades. A humble and soft-spoken champion of children, particularly the troubled and underachieving, she routinely spends hours working with parents and teachers to find innovative ways to help each child. Though sometimes maligned for her convictions, she considered her work more of a calling than a job. When I asked her how she helped her staff to work with difficult children, she answered:

I've always told staff to take the approach that these children are in a state of trauma. Something has happened in their life. Think about where these children came from and the fact that they probably saw something in their lifetime that traumatized them. They've witnessed cruelty, a crime, beatings, perhaps a death, and they are so traumatized they can't handle it. These are the kids we really have to pay attention to. They are crying for help – they're acting out because they can't express what they feel and they are afraid of us. Truly, they're afraid of this structured, safe environment because they don't know any better. I beg all the teachers on our team: Get to know the students that are sitting in front of you. Don't try to teach them right away, not until you understand what their background is, what baggage they're coming in with. Try to understand what hurt them so that we can help them work through that here, because if you don't do that, who is going to?

That's a challenging question: If we don't help our children, who will? I'm reminded of the words of theologian Ravi Zacharias:

> What we need to understand more than anything else is that if our children and young people don't hear our voice, they will hear someone else's. The multiple

highways into a person's heart and soul today are almost too numerous to counter because they invade the imagination and violate reason at ages in which our young people are most vulnerable. The younger they are, and the more wrong-headed they become, the more difficult the salvage operation. Don't wait until they reach sixteen or seventeen, but start off young in teaching them how to think things through. Critical thinking is the best gift we can give them. I don't mean thinking that criticizes, but thinking that learns how to evaluate truth.[5]

That's the heart of it. In our age of relativism, there is still such a thing as truth. We have to start by being honest with ourselves about the division in our own hearts, about the apathy that prevents us from tackling a problem head-on. Then we need to bring our words and actions in line with our ideals. We should not be ashamed if it takes some hard work. If children are watching the struggle, they will also see the outcome. We may not get thanked for all our efforts. The rewards will come when our children rise to meet their own challenges and look back at us with respect and understanding.

Chapter 7

Guidance to Grow

Before I had children, I had six theories about bringing them up; now I have six children and no theories.

JOHN WILMOT,
EARL OF ROCHESTER

Discipline is probably the most misunderstood word in the vocabulary of both teaching and parenting. It is not a matter of control, suppression, or coercion – these are in fact the opposite of true discipline. What is it then? In the end it's nothing more than guiding children to choose right over wrong. It may include consequences, but it should never involve cruelty or corporal punishment.

Every child needs boundaries, and has to be guided back to them again and again. This is a worthy task, and the end result will be mature, dependable adults.

Over the centuries, discipline has shaped the best scientific and religious minds. Now it is our turn to guide children in the same direction.

True discipline is an act of love, not anger. It takes into consideration the inner disposition of the child. As my grandfather said, "Raising children should mean helping them to become what they already are in God's mind."

That was how my parents raised my sisters and me, and I thank God for the discipline that I received. It gave us a relationship of mutual love and trust that lasted, unbroken, to the end of their lives. Of course, it was grounded in plenty of old-fashioned correction, including loud fatherly reprimands if we were overheard "talking back" to our mother.

Name-calling and mockery were unacceptable in our house. Like kids anywhere, we sometimes made fun of adults whose idiosyncrasies made them stand out, like our neighbor Nicholas, who stuttered, and Gunther, an extremely tall school librarian. But even if our targets knew nothing of the ridicule that went on behind their backs, our parents failed to see any humor in it. They would not tolerate cruelty.

Still, even if a punishment was deserved, sometimes we received a hug instead. One time when I was

eight, I upset my father so much that he felt he had
no option but to spank me. As I waited for his hand
to fall, I looked up at him and, before I knew what I
was doing, blurted out, "Papa, I'm really sorry. Do
what you have to do – but I know you still love me."
To my astonishment, he leaned down, hugged me,
and said with a tenderness that came from the bottom
of his heart: "Christoph, I forgive you." My apology
had completely disarmed him.

Because this incident made me realize how much
my father loved me, it has always remained vivid
in my mind. It also taught me a lesson I have never
forgotten – one I drew on in dealing with my own
children years later: don't be afraid to discipline a
child, but the moment you feel he is sorry, be sure
there is immediate and complete forgiveness on your
part. A forgiving hug from mom or dad, especially at
times when a child knows he deserves a consequence,
can totally change the landscape. As in nature when
the sun breaks through the storm clouds, the knowledge that one's failings have been forgiven is probably
the most rewarding experience of childhood.

When disciplining a child, rushing into action often
causes regret later. It's worth taking time to consider;
there is a lot at stake. Ask yourself how you can reach

the child's heart so that she can recognize her error.
If you achieve this, the battle is won and the rewards
are great. Family counselor and writer Dorothy Law
Nolte expresses it well:

> If children live with criticism, they learn to condemn.
> If children live with hostility, they learn to fight. If
> children live with ridicule, they learn to be shy. If
> children live with shame, they learn to feel guilty. If
> children live with encouragement, they learn confi-
> dence. If children live with tolerance, they learn to
> be patient. If children live with praise, they learn to
> appreciate. If children live with acceptance, they learn
> to love. If children live with approval, they learn to
> like themselves. If children live with honesty, they
> learn truthfulness. If children live with security, they
> learn to have faith in themselves and others. If chil-
> dren live with friendliness, they learn the world can
> be a friendly place.[1]

I am hesitant, in these pages, to advise readers on
how to guide and discipline a child within the home;
after all, each child brings a unique set of strengths
and weaknesses, promises and challenges, as does
every parent. Perhaps it is best to follow the wisdom
of Janusz Korczak, a remarkable pediatrician whose
story is detailed later in this chapter. He writes:

You yourself are the child you must learn to know, rear, and above all enlighten. To demand that others should provide you with answers is like asking a strange woman to give birth to your baby. There are insights that can be born only of your own pain, and they are the most precious. Seek in your child the undiscovered part of yourself.[2]

Speaking of insights "born of pain," my wife and I gained several in the course of bringing up eight children. Like most parents, it is probably safe to say that there is plenty we would do differently if we had the chance to do it again. Sometimes we unfairly assumed bad motives; at other times we had the wool pulled over our eyes; one day we were too lenient; the next, too strict. But we did learn several basic lessons nonetheless.

Children can be amazingly strong-willed, as anyone with a two-year-old has experienced. To hold out firmly and consistently is often exasperating. It is easier to let things slide. Yet anyone who prefers comfort to the effort of demanding obedience will find that, in the long run, the problem will grow bigger and bigger.

Consider the story of a British general who walked his horse through a street corner again and again, until the stubborn mare turned the way he had taught it to. "Never give in till the battle is won," the general said after the nineteenth time, when the animal finally turned as he wished. Frustrating as the incident must have been, the lesson it contains is a vital one.

Perseverance is one of the greatest gifts we can give our children. They'll sense it from us as we help them learn to listen and follow directions, to keep trying when results are unsatisfactory. In this practical way we can model willpower, a survival trait in today's world. Teens who haven't acquired this drive are at great risk when it's time for them to step out and try something new.

While raising our children, we also learned the value of instilling honesty from the earliest years. When a child is conscious of having done something wrong, but there are no consequences, he finds out that he can get away with it. It is terrible for a child to get that message. When they are young, the issue might seem unimportant and the misdeed small. But it can have repercussions far into the future. The old saying, "Little children, little problems; big children, big problems," is easy enough to dismiss, yet it contains a significant truth. A six-year-old may only snitch cookies; at sixteen he may be shoplifting or misusing alcohol. And while the will of a small child may be guided with relative ease, a rebellious teenager can only be reined in with the most strenuous effort.

Despite the need for consequences, they are not sufficient in themselves. Discipline entails more than catching a child in the act and punishing him. Far more important is nurturing his will for the good, which means supporting him whenever he chooses right over wrong – or, as my mother used to put it, "winning him for the good." Such affirmation has nothing to do with manipulation; the purpose of raising children can never be to simply make them obey. Rather, our goal should always be to help them toward the confidence that enables them to explore life and yet know their limits. That is the best preparation for adulthood.

Writer Anthony Bloom was once asked by an interviewer what part of his upbringing stood out most clearly in his memory. He answered simply:

Two things my father said impressed me and have stayed with me all my life. One was this: I remember he said after a holiday, "I worried about you," and I said, "Did you think I'd had an accident?" He said, "That would have meant nothing . . . I thought you had lost your integrity." Then on another occasion he said to me, "Always remember that whether you

are alive or dead matters nothing. What matters is
what you live for and what you are prepared to die
for." These two things were the background of my
education.[3]

Bloom was lucky to have a father who inspired
integrity rather than tried to teach it, an important
distinction. Sometimes we distrust a child, or read
bad motives into his behavior, which can weaken him
by making him doubt himself. Constantly criticizing
and correcting a child will likewise discourage him.
Worse, it will take away the best reason he has to
trust in you: his confidence that you understand and
forgive him, and will let him start over.

It is surely important, when a child has been
dishonest, to get to the facts of what happened and
to encourage the child to face up to them. But it is
rarely good to probe into the child's motives, and
always wrong to push for a confession. After all, it
may be nothing more than embarrassment or shame
that caused the child to wriggle out of something by
means of a half-truth to begin with, and if pressed, he
may be so afraid of the consequences that he will tell
an outright lie. Don't adults do that, too, for the very
same reasons?

Naturally, every child needs correction regularly.
But if we react too strongly, the ultimate purpose

of correction – helping the child to make a fresh start – is overshadowed by the discipline itself. It's better to give a child the benefit of the doubt.

There's no question that being a friend and companion as well as a parent requires double the patience and energy. But as Dale – the attorney who gave up his job to be a father – notes, there are few things as satisfying:

> When I think about it, it is much easier to live with children who fear you than it is to live with children who love you, because if your children fear you, when you come home they're gone. They scatter. They go to their rooms and shut the door, and you make it easier for them by piling their rooms full of computers, sound systems, and everything else. But if you have children who love you, you can't get them out of your hair! They're hanging on to your legs, they're pulling on your trousers, you come home and they want your attention. You sit down, they're all over your lap. You feel like a walking jungle gym. You also feel loved.

The willingness to be vulnerable is an important part of parenting. Few experiences brought us as close to our children as the times we overreacted, but realized it and asked them to forgive us. Every day must be a new day, the past completely forgiven. No matter

what they are going through, they should always
feel the assurance that we are ready to stand by
them – not hovering nervously over them, but staying
solidly at their side.

Obviously, every family has its ups and downs,
trying moments, and embarrassing dramas. There
is nothing as complex as the relationship between
a parent and a child. But there is also nothing as
beautiful. And that is what we need to hold on to
whenever we reach the end of our rope. As psychologist Theodor Reik says: "Romance fails us and so do
friendships, but the relationship of parent and child,
less noisy than all others, remains indelible and inde-
structible, the strongest relationship on earth."

After parents, the relationship of greatest influence
is often that of teacher and child. I've always felt that
teachers have the toughest and most rewarding job on
the planet. To quote Carl Jung:

> One looks back with appreciation to the brilliant
> teachers, but with gratitude to those who touched our
> human feelings. The curriculum is so much necessary
> raw material, but warmth is the vital element for the
> growing plant and for the soul of the child.

I've never met anyone who didn't have a story
to tell about a teacher who affected his or her life

powerfully. Maureen, an editor and a mother of three, told me that she looks back to her second grade year as an anchor-point in her life.

We were a wild stampede of a class that no teacher could control. Richard Wareham, already in his sixties, was called out of semi-retirement to see what he could do.

When our class tried to take this grandpa for a ride, we were reined in fast, and he did it without raising his voice or sending us to the principal. He came at conflicts from an unexpected angle. If two kids were fighting, he assigned them to clean opposite sides of a school window. From one second to another, enemies went from glaring furiously past each other to giggling foolishly and synchronizing their rags through the glass.

If there were rumblings of mutiny in the class, Richard would preempt it by throwing his bandana into the air. While it was airborne, we knew we were authorized to erupt in a group shout. The second it hit the floor there had to be utter silence. Anyone unable or unwilling to cease the noise found himself out on the school lawn, digging up dandelions. Other pressure-release mechanisms included orienteering and bird-watching, building a lean-to clubhouse, and creating a complex obstacle course.

But his greatest legacy was his love and respect
for each child. Once he reprimanded me sternly for
a prank I had (for a change) not committed. I was
angry and tearful at his allegation. He listened to
my side of the story, apologized for his mistake, and
pointed out that in life, people may often misunder-
stand or criticize your actions. "If they are wrong,"
he told me, "don't lash out. Hold up your head and
keep doing what's right. Show them, don't tell them."
I was seven at the time, but I've never forgotten it.

More than a teacher, Richard was a training coach for
student teachers and a counselor for parents. While
battling cancer, he took time to write down some of his
core teaching discoveries, which since have circulated
through many families and classrooms. He wrote:

Each child should be taught, at home and at school,
some simple values that will help him all through
life. These values cannot be substituted for or
replaced by high-powered programs or by positive
reinforcements such as special trips, treats, or favors.
Nor can we expect these values to suddenly appear
out of the blue when the child is in high school.
Our chance to teach these values comes at home, in
kindergarten, in school, each day, in each situation –
and no two situations are alike.

No. A clear, firm, no-option "no." In order for a child to experience the value of "no," he has to know that it means no argument, no nagging, no alternative, no nonsense. When "no" is said, that is what is meant!

Come. This is my starting point. "Come" has to mean "come," otherwise we can't even gather. If there is no gathering, children will quickly go their own way and find chaos and confusion nearby. A gathered experience is shared and appreciated by all.

Listen. Full attention is a special blessing. If a child has assumed the right to turn you off and tune in elsewhere by his own choice, the generation gap has already begun, and your heart-to-heart contact will have to be won anew. Speak when listening is at your door.

Quiet. There are times when it makes my heart glad to hear thirteen children all talking at once. A teacher or parent can learn a lot from multiple parallel subjects! But children need to experience times of quiet, and the satisfaction of being quietly occupied, alone. This is of special importance for the super-active child whose "programming" rises higher and higher until he can't turn it off, and nothing can hold his interest anymore.

Wait. There is much waiting in life, sometimes short, sometimes much longer. We teach impatience if we don't help our children to wait peacefully.

Care. We must help children learn to be responsible in all they do. This includes work, play, care of equipment and clothing, relationships with others, respect, and much more. We *can* expect responsibility from them.

To me, Richard's short list contains a lot of wisdom. His respect for the spirit of childhood inspired him to want the best for each of his charges, so his teaching became a bequest for their future. No question, this is an enormously difficult task when a teacher is confronted with troubled and rebellious students. Still, we serve as signposts to direct them forward, on a road where they may not encounter many other trustworthy guides.

Often it seems that every day brings another headline highlighting our society's distrust of – and disrespect toward – children. It's up to teachers to hold onto passion and compassion in the face of these actions born of fear. Recently, the *New York Times* published an editorial called "Giving Up on Four-Year-Olds":

A new report released by the Department of Education's Office for Civil Rights, examining the disciplinary practices of the country's 97,000 public schools, shows that excessively punitive policies are being used at every level of the public school system – even against four-year-olds in preschool. This should shame the nation and force it to re-evaluate the destructive measures that schools are using against their most vulnerable children.

Black students, for example, are suspended at three times the rate of white students. Minority children with disabilities fare worst of all; the race effect is amplified when disability comes into the picture. . . .

The fact that minority children at age four are already being disproportionately suspended or expelled is an outrage. The pattern of exclusion suggests that schools are giving up on these children when they are barely out of diapers. It runs counter to the very mission of early education. . . . It harms children emotionally at an age when they are incapable of absorbing lessons from this form of punishment. And it places those children at greater risk of falling behind, dropping out, or becoming permanently involved with the juvenile justice system.[4]

It's appalling that children of any age are singled out by their race or disability. If anything, their

vulnerable circumstances, as well as their youth,
should evoke extra care and patience. In some
schools, behavioral problems that used to be
addressed by teachers and guidance counselors are
now being handled by law enforcement. Young children are being suspended or forcibly removed from
the premises simply for having a tantrum, or for
being unruly. This, too, is an attack on childhood.

Should a four-year-old have a rap sheet following
him through his school years, telling him he's a delinquent until he finally becomes one? Too many of our
country's young people are behind bars because those
who should have cared for them gave up too soon.
What does it say about a society when its policymakers bet on the failure of the next generation, and
no one protests? What does it say about the way we
view children, when we allow the guardians of their
future to expel them before they can write their
names?

Clearly, a comprehensive discussion of these
concerns is beyond the scope of this book. But surely
awareness is the first step, and speaking out in the
public arena is another. These trends can only be
reversed by grassroots action.

Earlier in this chapter I referred to Janusz Korczak, whose writings on children are revered throughout Europe. Korczak was a Polish-Jewish teacher, children's author, and doctor whose selfless devotion to orphans in the Warsaw Ghetto earned him the title "King of Children." He never tired of reminding people how it felt to be a child in an adult world, and emphasized the importance of educating children not "from the head" but "from the heart."

Korczak's insistence on what he called "standing with the child" was not only a principle. On August 6, 1942, as the two hundred orphans under his care were rounded up and loaded onto trains headed for the gas chambers of Treblinka, Korczak refused the last-minute offers of Gentile friends who arranged for his escape and chose instead to accompany his charges on the ride that carried them to their deaths.

Few stories of devotion are as stirring as Korczak's. Our circumstances may be different, yet despite the distance between his era and ours, far too many children in the world today suffer for want of even one such guardian – one adult who will take them by the hand and stick with them, come what may. And so for us, who live in a time of relative peace and prosperity, Korczak's last recorded words not only remind us of his heroism, but stand as a challenge to each of us who has ever cared for a child: "You do not leave sick children in the night," he said. "And you do not leave them in a time like this."

Chapter 8

In Praise of Difficult Children

The lost child cries,
but still he catches fireflies.

Y O S H I D A   R Y U S U I

In a culture teeming with opportunities to compete, it's easy enough to find teen pop queens, academic prodigies, and precocious young CEOs.

But there are other stories that don't always make the news. They're the stories of the developmentally disabled, the dropouts, and the juvenile offenders. There's the quiet pain of the obese, the awkward, and the slow. There's the epidemic of the hyperactive, the medicated, and the depressed. So many children lack hope, not necessarily because there's anything wrong with them, but simply because they've been made to feel that they're losers.

Never has childhood been such a lonely, joyless voyage for so many. One could almost say that childhood itself is now viewed as a suspect phase in human development. Children of all ages are being censured, on the playground and in class, simply because they're behaving as children should. Often diagnosed with "problems" that used to be considered normal childhood traits – impulsiveness and exuberance, spontaneity and daring – millions of children are being diagnosed as hyperactive and drugged into submission. I'm referring, of course, to the widespread use of Ritalin, Adderall, and similar drugs, and to the public's fascination with medicine as the answer to any and every problem.

And Ritalin is only one drug of many now being used to control and suppress children: equally worrying (and even more toxic) are the antidepressants, mood stabilizers, and antipsychotics being prescribed to children as well.

Prescription drugs may be appropriate for certain specific conditions. But given the diagnostic explosion (the United States accounts for five percent of the world's population, and eighty-five percent of its Ritalin use)[1] one has to wonder if they aren't overused. Too many children receive them as a first option, rather than a last resort. Once they're on, they often stay on. And when children get prescription drugs, they run the risk of becoming addicted for life. Many schools require screening programs for attention-deficit hyperactivity disorder in children and teenagers, generating even more drug sales.

Critics such as Peter Breggin contend that often ADHD is nothing more than a defense against over-structuring – a natural reflex that used to be called letting off steam – or alternately, a symptom of various unmet emotional needs. Breggin, a pediatrician, writes:

> People call drugs like Ritalin a godsend for emotional and behavioral problems . . . but I think the way they're overused is absolutely horrifying. When I was asked by the National Institute of Health to be a scientific discussant on the effects of these drugs. . . . I reviewed the important literature, and I found that when animals are given them, they stop playing; they stop being curious; they stop social-izing; they stop trying to escape. Ritalin makes good caged animals . . . we're making good caged kids. It's all very well to talk about it taking a whole village to raise a child, but in practice, we're acting as if we think it only takes a pill.[2]

Whether or not ADHD is a valid diagnosis at all remains a matter of ongoing controversy; one camp portrays it as a diagnosable disease, while the other

says it too easily describes almost all normal children.
But most parents and teachers who deal with it on a
daily basis would not hesitate to describe it as challenging and exhausting. There is no question that the
diagnosis of ADHD fuels a billion-dollar industry of
psychiatrists, behavioral therapists, and drug manu-
facturers. But it is also true that increasing numbers
of children are displaying behavior that is so disrup-
tive on a daily basis that their parents and teachers are
driven to doctors for help, because they cannot get
help anywhere else.

Considering how many children today struggle to
find a stable footing, we need to find a new approach
to early intervention. I know that for parents, it's a
relief to know that a child's difficulties are recognized
and understood. Sometimes naming a problem is the
beginning of getting help. Other times, it effectively
sidelines bright and capable children into special
needs and slow learner classrooms. The burgeoning
number of diagnoses makes it difficult for even the
most dedicated teachers to determine each child's
gifts and limitations.

If we are misled into thinking that children's
destructive behavior always represents some type of
disease, and give them medication which is potentially

dangerous, then we are taking the easy way out. Instead, we could look at our homes and schools and recognize how often our own busyness and materialism prevent children from finding inner peace and emotional stability. Sara Barnett, a social worker, tells this story:

> When I worked in an outpatient clinic, parents would often bring their kids in with a generic complaint like, "He doesn't follow directions," or, "He's having too many temper tantrums." There's this label that you can give kids called "disruptive behavior disorder" which just means they act out, or they don't follow directions.
>
> Part of an evidence-based treatment for this is called "parent-child interactive therapy." The first part of the therapy requires the parent to spend five minutes a day playing with their child. Five minutes a day! Many parents were unwilling, and I heard a whole list of excuses of why it wasn't possible. One of the major reasons I left that job, after the birth of my daughter, was that I could not fathom how a parent couldn't spend five minutes a day with their child.
>
> Clinically speaking, the disruptive behavior can be traced back to not having proper attachment with the parents. You're not going to listen to your parent if there's no dialogue. They think, "Why should I listen

to your directive to me? It doesn't mean anything; it doesn't hold any power over me." I would explain this to parents and they would say, "Yes, yes, yes." But they didn't want to do the work; they wanted to bring their kid to me to fix. It's heartbreaking.

There are many causes for children's instability. While we can't resolve all of them at once, we do have some say in our own family or classroom. So let's start there. Even five minutes a day is a beginning. Reversing the trend will certainly not be easy. But the longer we hesitate, the more children will grow up struggling under a heavy burden. Having that burden labelled does not always lighten the load; in fact, it can cause parents, teachers, and even peers to respond to the label instead of the child.

We need to help each child to do his best with what he has, while addressing his specific challenges. Take the story of Kyle, as told by his mother Irene:

> Kyle was six when diagnosed with ADHD. When we read the list of symptoms, we knew it was a match: easily distracted, has difficulty playing quietly, talks excessively, has trouble waiting for his or her turn, blurts out answers before the question has been completed, is impulsive, squirms, fidgets, or bounces when sitting, has problems concentrating – that was

Kyle all over. But did this mean he had a disability? We wondered who was drawing these mysterious lines between disabled and normal.

Born early, Kyle was a sleepy child who barely opened his eyes. At three months he woke up and began life on high octane. He fussed in his crib unless a new toy or mobile was produced. He never snuggled with a stuffed animal and didn't like to sit on laps. He began taking steps at nine months and was running at one year. When given a puzzle, he dumped it out and completed it quickly, using both hands.

Words and full sentences spilled from his mouth like a waterfall. He was always busy, getting into everything, and appropriating the other children's toys. In childcare, his teacher told us, "If I'm not a step ahead of Kyle, he's two steps ahead of me." At three years old, he ran ahead of his class and climbed a very high tree to explore a tree house, while his teacher searched for him everywhere. Always running, jumping, or climbing, he broke his collarbone twice.

In first grade, he rebelled against the routine of the schedule. He misbehaved and broke rules. He didn't have many friends. He was frustrated. We were frustrated. It seemed no matter what we tried, nothing worked. Except being outside.

On weekends, Kyle spent hours observing bugs or climbing trees and sitting in the branches watching

the birds. He discovered nests and began collecting
them, learning the different birds' ways. Listening to
recordings, he memorized their songs and on family
walks he would identify the birds correctly before
even seeing them.

Summer brought the joy of sleeping out in the
backyard, making campfires, roasting marshmal-
lows, drifting to sleep under millions of stars. His
father helped him make a little boat, and they spent
hours sailing it along rushing streams. We must have
hiked and biked hundreds of miles, just keeping up
with Kyle.

But fall always came around. Kyle had to return
to the classroom desk, the overstimulation, the
demands. We decided to take action. Working with
his teachers and our family doctor, we came up with a
battle plan.

We started by de-cluttering his room and desk area
at school. We took away many pictures, toys, books,
and games, leaving space for bird's nests, seashells,
and driftwood. We toned down the color scheme in
his room, removing anything bright and applying
earth colors instead.

We cut back on activities: in the evenings after
a busy school day, we came home to unwind by
reading in a tree house or on the sofa, instead of
playing ball. We no longer accepted every invitation

to other people's houses. We politely told them that we already had plans – not to hurt anyone's feelings, but our plans were to stay quietly at home!

If a birthday or camping trip was coming up, we didn't tell him too far ahead of time – the expectation was not worth the over-excitement. We kept to a regular schedule as much as possible, the same routine every day. And we made a pact to give positive encouragement whenever he succeeded, rather than negative when he didn't (even if the latter happened more often). In short, we took life day by day, moment by moment, which is actually how a child lives.

In the end, nature was always the most effective medicine. One winter day, he was sitting quietly, feeding a chickadee on his open hand. A school visitor asked how he had managed to tame the bird. His wise teacher remarked, "Kyle didn't tame the bird, the bird tamed him."

To all the parents who are struggling to help their unique child find a route forward, just keep going, and don't stop loving. Kyle went on to a successful career in computer science. He is happily married with two small children, and has recently bought a house complete with a big back yard full of trees so his kids can find their footing in nature as he did.

Irene's family was lucky – their family doctor and
school were inspired to team up with them on Kyle's
behalf. If only that could happen for every child.
Perhaps doctors' and therapists' offices should
display a plaque: "Any diagnosis should be viewed
only as an aid in understanding the challenges this
child faces, to discover how best to support him
or her." Each child has difficulties, but whether
these lead to fulfilment or disaster is largely up to
us adults – a huge responsibility. It may help us to
consider how hard it is to define a child as "normal."
Is there such a thing? Instead of categorizing abnor-
mality at an early age, we could then be freed to focus
on the roots of change: healthier environments, less
rigid expectations, more flexible teaching.

As a child, Temple Grandin was diagnosed as
profoundly autistic. Through sheer grit, along with
the encouragement of her mother and a visionary
science teacher, she went on to become a scien-
tist, professor, author, inventor, and tireless activist
for children who learn differently. In a talk titled
"The World Needs All Kinds of Minds," Grandin
addressed the cultural tendency to assume that with
education, one size should fit all:

Autism is a very broad spectrum and diagnosis is not precise. It's a behavioral profile, a continuum of traits. . . . Half is science, and half is doctors squabbling around conference tables. There's another term, social communication disorder, which they say is different from autism. There's also "pervasive developmental disorder, not otherwise specified." What is that? Kids are labeled Asperger's, ADHD, or heaven forbid, oppositional-defiant – that's just the worst. Any kid is going to turn oppositional-defiant if they're not motivated.

We've got to show kids that there are interesting things out there to motivate them. Different kinds of minds have got to work together. I'm getting very concerned that our educational system is forgetting about the visual thinkers, the mathematic thinkers. Things are getting way too verbal. . . . Schools are taking out the visual thinking and hands-on classes. They don't test for mechanical aptitude. Hands-on learning is what saved me. The "quirky, nerdy" kids are the creativity for the future. . . . I'm concerned that this country is eating its educational seed corn.[3]

Grandin went on to point out that according to today's framework for diagnosis, geniuses like Mozart, Tesla, and Einstein would probably all be diagnosed with some form of autism. After all, Einstein didn't speak till he was three.

Einstein is one of my heroes, not as much for his scientific brilliance as for his wisdom and humility. He often spoke up for true learning: "I am neither very clever nor especially gifted. I am only very, very curious!" On two other occasions, he wrote:

> The important thing is not to stop questioning. Curiosity has its own reason for existence. One cannot help but be in awe when one contemplates the mysteries of eternity, of life, of the marvelous structure of reality. It is enough if one tries to comprehend a little of this mystery each day. Never lose a holy curiosity.

> I sometimes ask myself, how did it happen that I was the one to develop the theory of relativity? The reason, I think, is that a normal adult never stops to think about problems of space and time. These are things which he has thought of as a child. But my intellectual development was retarded, as a result of which I began to wonder about space and time only when I had already grown up.[4]

Einstein speaks of feeling out of step with expectations. Every family, every class, has that kid, who's prone to stretch limits or take things "too far," who's embarrassingly honest, who's always in trouble. It's that child over whom every teacher puzzles longest and every parent loses the most sleep. No matter how natural the phenomenon, being a misfit is never easy. Janine, a woman who suffered finger-pointing and rejection for years, says:

> Even as a very young child I always told people exactly what I thought, though this was seldom appreciated. If someone had a blemish on their face, if they hobbled or snuffled or had a nervous twitch, I always pointed it out. If I would see an adult who looked depressed, I would ask them what was wrong. And of course I was always reprimanded.
>
> I'm grateful that much of my childhood is a blur now, but I can never forget the feeling of being the misfit – always in trouble, and always accused of creating trouble. In school, an exclusive private one, I stole, cheated, and lied. I stuck to myself a lot, and when I felt picked on I could be mean. But I was also very insecure. It didn't help that I was labeled early on, especially by a particular teacher, as the one to watch out for. That reputation followed me wherever I went, and helped people assume that I was always about to act out. The subs at school were all advised, "Watch out for her, that's why she's in the front row." I lied to keep out of trouble, then got caught and lied more.

By the time I left school, I had given up on myself.
Why not? No one else seemed to believe in me.
Though frustrated, I steeled myself against every
emotion and became a walking stone. I couldn't cry
for years.

Looking back on my childhood now, I'm sure I
was not without guilt. I probably was a difficult child
in many respects. But should a kid ever feel given
up on, or marked to the point where she despairs?
Isn't it the right of every child to feel that someone
believes in her, and that things can indeed change?

While the tribulations of a woman like Janine may
seem negligible compared to physical and sexual
abuse, they are not. As her story shows, the weight of
a negative label can be just as impossible for a child to
carry. In any case, the emotional suffering of a child
is never insignificant. Because they are so vulnerable,
and because they are dependent on the adults around
them, children are, in my experience, far more sensitive
to criticism than one might guess, and far more easily
crushed. And even if their natural forgetfulness and
their amazing capacity to forgive relieves most children
of much that might burden an adult, there are those
whose self-confidence can be shattered by an unjust
accusation, a cutting remark, or a hasty miscalculation.

Whenever we pass judgment on a child, we fail to see him as a whole person. True, he may be nervous, shy, stubborn, or violent; we may know his siblings or his background, or think we recognize family traits. But that is stereotyping. To focus on any one aspect of a child, especially a negative one, is to put him in a box whose sides may not really be determined by reality, but only by our own expectations. And to categorize him as a result is to forget that his destiny was not placed in our hands. It may also limit his potential and thus the person he will become.

Comparing children – whether our own or other people's – is just as bad as labeling them. Obviously, every child is different. Some seem to get all the lucky breaks, while others have a rough time simply coping with life. One child consistently brings home perfect scores, while the next is always at the bottom of the class. Another is gifted and popular, while still another, no matter how hard he tries, is always in trouble. Children must be brought up to accept these facts. But as parents, and educators, we must do our part, too, and refrain from showing favoritism, and from comparing our children with others. Above all, we must refrain from pushing them to become something that their unique personal makeup may never allow them to be.

A child's abilities should never be stifled or ignored. Yet there are also dangers in encouraging them too much. Praise should be based on hard work and improvement, not on a child's inherent gifts. It is no small task to guide a child who has been made overly conscious of her talents, and when this is the result of flattery, it is even harder. Add to that an exaggerated notion of self-worth, which is almost always acquired at the expense of others, and you have a child who may have great difficulty relating to her peers.

It is the same with the extra attention and subtle favoritism given to children whose physical attractiveness, sunny smiles, and easy-going personalities allow them to glide through childhood. My grandfather pointed out that such children are saddled with a "golden curse" – the dangerous illusion that because everything and everyone favored them in childhood, the adult world will treat them the same way.

As parents and teachers, we may also confuse "good" children with merely "easy" ones. Raising a good child is a dubious goal in the first place, if only because the line between instilling integrity and breeding self-righteousness is so fine. As educator Thomas Lickona has pointed out, getting into trouble can be a vital part of building a child's character:

You want to encourage obedience, but you don't want to stifle independence. It's wisely been said that every child should have the confidence to misbehave occasionally. Giving kids room to be less than perfect is important. . . . The girl who's a "little angel" as a child isn't necessarily the one who'll make a resourceful, independent adult.[5]

While excessive praise can harm a "good" child, the negative comparisons that leave another one feeling that he is "bad" can be downright devastating. That is because as long as we compare the "bad" child's qualities to those of the "good" one, we tie his self-esteem to his ability to keep up with someone else, and thus trap him in a cycle of endless frustration and self-doubt.

As a parent, I've often thought of Korczak's simple words: "I am convinced that there is ten times more good than bad in a child, and about the bad, we can wait and see." As a speaker at schools, I have shared the following words, written by a group of students, with countless children. To me, they express in a child's language all the positive messages that can get lost in the struggle to "just get through the day":

You are very special. In all the world, there is nobody like you. Since the beginning of time, nobody has had your smile, your eyes, your hands, your hair. Nobody owns your voice, your handwriting, your way of communicating with others. Nobody paints like you, or has your tastes. Nobody sees things as you do. Nobody has ever laughed or cried exactly like you.

Nobody else in the world has your particular set of abilities. There will always be someone who is better at one thing or another. Every person is your superior in at least one way. But nobody in this world has your specific combination of talents and feelings. And because of that, no one will ever love, walk, talk, think, or act exactly like you.

Whatever is rare or unique has enormous value, and it's the same with you. You are no accident – God made you for a special purpose. God gave you a task and purpose that nobody else can do as well as you can. Out of billions of applicants, only one is qualified. Only one has the right combination of what it takes – and that one is you.[6]

Whenever I read these words to children, the response is beautiful to see. They are reminded that their lives have meaning, regardless of their shortcomings or struggles.

It is often hard for parents to see the benefits of having raised a difficult child – even when the outcome is positive. For some, the heartache has simply taken too big a toll; for others, the sense of relief is so great that, once the battle is over, neither parent nor child ever chooses to mention it again. But strange as it may sound, I believe that the more challenging the child, the more grateful the parent should be. If anything, parents of difficult children ought to be envied, because it is they, more than any others, who are forced to learn the most wonderful secret of true parenthood: the meaning of unconditional love. It is a secret that remains hidden from those whose love is never tested.

When we welcome the prospect of raising the problematic child with these things in mind, we will begin to see our frustrations as moments that can awaken our best qualities. And instead of envying the ease with which our neighbors seem to raise perfect offspring, we will remember that rule-breakers and children who show their horns often make more self-reliant and independent adults than those whose limits are never tried. In the words of Henry Ward Beecher, the nineteenth-century social reformer, abolitionist, and preacher: "The energy that makes a child hard to manage is the energy that afterwards makes him a manager of life." And even if the trials of our own childhood leave us hesitant to embrace

such a positive view, we can always look away from
ourselves and to our children. In loving and being
loved by them we will always rediscover the power of
forgiving, the importance of leaving the past behind,
and the optimism born of hope.

Forgiveness is necessary dozens of times a day.
No matter how many times a child gets into trouble,
never lose faith in him. To label a child as hopeless
is to be tempted by despair, and to the extent that
despair is a lack of hope, it is also a lack of love. If we
truly love our children, we may at times throw up
our hands in desperation, but we will never give up
on them. God sent the Hebrews not only the Law of
Moses but also manna, the bread of heaven. Without
such bread – that is, without warmth, humor, kindness, and compassion – no family can survive.

Instead of hushing up the children who embarrass
us, instead of clamping down on the ones who don't
fit in, instead of analyzing the troubled ones and
drawing conclusions about their delinquent futures,
we need to welcome them all as they are. By helping
us to discover the limitations of "goodness" and the
boredom of conformity, they can teach us the necessity of genuineness, the wisdom of humility, and
the reality that, in parenting and education as with
anything else, nothing good is won without struggle.

Chapter 9

Discovering Reverence

When a child walks down the road,
a company of angels goes before him
proclaiming, "Make way for the image
of the Holy One."

HASIDIC SAYING

In a society overwhelmed by countless problems, the greatest dangers to children are obvious: poverty, violence, neglect, disease, abuse, and countless other ills. But what can any one of us do to overcome them? In an essay on the question of social renewal, Hermann Hesse suggests that the first step is to recognize their root cause: our lack of reverence for life.

All disrespect, all irreverence, all hardheartedness, all contempt is nothing else than killing. And it is possible to kill not only what is in the present, but also that which is in the future. With just a little witty skepticism we can kill a good deal of the future in a

child or young person. Life is waiting everywhere,
flowering everywhere, but we only see a small part of
it and trample much of it with our feet.[1]

Hesse touches on something that endangers children
more than anything else in the world today. Irreverence for children pervades almost everything in a
culture that glorifies sex and violence at the expense of
innocence and gentleness. While no one is unaffected
by this destructive bent, the greatest victims are always
children. Often it seems that they are not given the
chance to grow up at all – they are thrown into adult
life before their hearts are able to distinguish between
what is good and what is glamorous. They end up
copying the worst of adult behavior without knowing
what they are doing. They may not be grown up, but
they are no longer truly children either.

Child advocate Diane Levin highlights the source
of much of this contamination:

After a week of school vacation, a teacher held a
group meeting with the six- and seven-year-old children in her class. When she asked them to share their
favorite activity from their vacation, all the children
gave a media example. For the boys, it was playing
video games, often violent ones. For the girls, it was
mostly viewing the current female performers popular

with young girls. When the teacher asked the children what they would have done on vacation if they didn't have any screens to use, they stared at her blankly. . . .

A decline in social skills can be amplified when combined with the media's message of violence, aggression, and mean-spirited behavior as well as sex, sexualization, and focus on appearance. The media culture frequently supports a stereotypical view that, for girls, the basis of relationships is how they look and the things they have, rather than their connection to others. And media culture teaches boys to judge themselves and one another based on how strong, independent, and ready to fight they are, not by their positive connection with others. In a sense, both boys and girls are made into objects. Objectification of self and others makes it much easier to act in mean and uncaring ways in relationships.[2]

When children sense they are being treated as objects, why shouldn't they respond accordingly? It's as if all that is wonderful, unique, and miraculous in each life is brought down to the lowest common denominator, gender. Without a clear sense of self, they can have no appreciation of who they are or how they came into being. Then they are fed a new, perverse interpretation of what it means to be male or female.

This promotes the formation of cliques, which often leads to bullying. Boys tend to take on a false manliness, a macho swagger that hides (at least from themselves) collective cowardice. Girls' cliques can be equally damaging in their exclusiveness and cruel pressure to conform. Worse, these children are prematurely burdened with adult sexuality.

Shaina, the mother of a teen, addresses this corrupted definition of girlhood:

> When the latest open-faced teenybopper queen hit the screen, my daughter was eleven years old. I was working late hours, and rarely had time to watch TV and gauge the positive messages of the show. But my daughter's friends' moms all assured me that this one gave good vibes, didn't dress like a slut, sang songs with lyrics any parent could approve, had a great relationship with her father, et cetera. I let my daughter aboard the bandwagon – not sure I could have kept her off it.
>
> When my daughter was wearing the outfits, singing the songs, dancing the moves, endlessly analyzing every show with her friends, fame caught up with the young performer. She disappeared in a flurry of drug charges, compromising photographs, bribes, and lies. When she resurfaced, she'd rein-vented herself with the hooker look, sound, and

act. And she was dragging all her "wholesome girl" worshippers along with her.

I ached for her as much as for my own kid. She should not have been on a stage at age twelve. Her parents should not have put her there, and I should not have let my kid watch. Fame eats children up, without apology or explanation. There are no good role models in that scene; they turn into suicide bombs, taking all the bystanders along.

So many features of our "advanced civilization" seem bent on destroying the spirit of childhood. Be it materialism, prescription drugs, standardized testing, technological devices, or the debased sensationalism that passes for entertainment, all of it harms children.

I believe that at birth, all children bear the stamp of their Creator. Their purity and innocence is a great gift. Once it has been lost, it cannot be replaced. All the more, it must be guarded as a treasure which no one has a right to destroy.

If we are going to protect innocence in a child, we need to cleanse our own hearts of pollution. Author Magda von Hattinberg once said:

I always feel that we keep our childhood locked inside, in a hidden cabinet. We carry it with us, and we see it most clearly in those moments when we are

able to feel passionately responsive to children. Some
people, I think, have buried their childhood, or they
have done something terrible: they have murdered it.
These are the sad characters one sees passing by an
innocent face and open little arms with indifference;
or else with a bad conscience.[3]

Our response upon encountering a child must be
nothing less than reverence. Perhaps because the
word sounds old-fashioned, its true meaning has been
blurred. Reverence is more than just love. It includes
an appreciation for the qualities children possess
(and which we ourselves have lost), a readiness to
rediscover their value, and the humility to learn from
them.

Reverence is also an attitude of deep respect, as
expressed by the following words of my grandfather:

It is children who lead us to the truth. We are not
worthy to educate even one of them. Our lips are
unclean; our dedication is not wholehearted. Our
truthfulness is partial; our love divided. Our kindness
is not without motives. We ourselves are not yet free
of lovelessness, possessiveness, and selfishness. Only
sages and saints – only those who stand as children
before God – are really fit to live and work with
children.[4]

Few of us dare count ourselves as sages or saints. Yet that is exactly why the basis of education must not only be knowledge and understanding, but reverence as well. In Erich Maria Remarque's novel *The Road Back,* written shortly after World War I, there is a passage that illustrates this belief in an unforgettable way. The speaker is Ernst, a veteran of combat in the trenches:

> Morning comes. I go to my class. There sit the little ones with folded arms. In their eyes is still all the shy astonishment of the childish years. They look up at me so trustingly, so believingly – and suddenly I get a spasm over the heart.
>
> Here I stand before you, one of the hundreds of thousands of bankrupt men in whom the war destroyed every belief and almost every strength. Here I stand before you, and see how much more alive, how much more rooted in life you are than I. . . . Shall I tell you that in twenty years you will be dried-up and crippled, your freest impulses maimed and pressed mercilessly into the selfsame mold? Should I tell you that all learning, all culture, all science is nothing but hideous mockery, so long as mankind makes war in the name of God and humanity with gas, iron, explosive, and fire? What

should I teach you then, you little creatures who
alone have remained unspotted by the terrible years?

   ... Should I tell you how to pull the string of
a hand grenade, how to best throw it at a human
being? Should I show you how to stab a man with
a bayonet ...? Should I demonstrate how best to
aim a rifle at such an incomprehensible miracle as a
breathing breast, a living heart? ...

   I stand here before you, a polluted, a guilty man
and can only implore you ever to remain as you are,
never to suffer the bright light of your childhood
to be misused as a blow flame of hate. About your
brows still blows the breath of innocence. How
then should I presume to teach you? Behind me,
still pursuing, are the bloody years. How then can I
venture among you? Must I not first become a child
again myself?

   I feel a cramp begin to spread through me, as
if I were turning to stone, as if I were crumbling
away.... "Children," I say with difficulty, "you may
go now. There will be no school today."

   The little ones look at me to make sure I am not
joking. I nod once again. "Yes, that is right – go
and play today – the whole day. Go and play in the
wood – or with your dogs and your cats – you need
not come back till tomorrow."[5]

Try doing something similar in a real classroom, and one would be questioned, if not fired. But the point, as Remarque makes clear, is not the incident itself. What is significant here is that the heart of a man is touched by a spirit our age has completely lost. He recognizes, when faced with innocence and vulnerability, honesty and spontaneity, that the only fitting response is reverence.

Understanding reverence can change our perception of the world and our task in it. This simple word can help us keep our own lives clear of entanglements that may try to drag us down. With the knowledge that a young audience is watching our every move, we can be models of integrity and respect. We can dress in a manner that expresses our inner worth, instead of degrading it. Instead of bombarding young children with explicit information about sexuality and reproduction, we can let them grow at their own pace into an understanding of what it means to be a human being, and answer questions honestly and simply as they arise.

We can model healthy relationships. I learned the importance of this from my own parents, who could disagree with each other quite openly, but always ended the debate with a laugh and a hug. I saw that

my father was not ashamed to show tenderness and
that my mother's gentle guidance was backed up with
enormous courage. Their marriage, built on faithful-
ness and respect, was an example to all who knew
them.

Once we have reverence for every life, we will also
have compassion, and teach others its value. Even the
most hardened and distant child can learn empathy,
and it is amazing to watch it happen. That's what
Mary Gordon discovered when she founded Roots
of Empathy, a program that brings babies into classrooms, with remarkable effects in reduced bullying,
greater understanding, and more caring. She writes:

> Darren was the oldest child I ever saw in a Roots
> of Empathy class. He was in eighth grade and had
> been held back twice. He was two years older than
> everyone else and already starting to grow a beard.
> I knew his story: his mother had been murdered in
> front of his eyes when he was four years old, and he
> had lived in a succession of foster homes ever since.
> Darren looked menacing because he wanted us to
> know he was tough: his head was shaved except for a
> ponytail at the top and he had a tattoo on the back of
> his head.
>
> The instructor of the Roots of Empathy program
> was explaining to the class about differences in

temperament. She invited the young mother who was visiting the class with Evan, her six-month-old baby, to share her thoughts about her baby's temperament. Joining in the discussion, the mother told the class how Evan liked to face outwards when he was in the baby carrier, how he didn't want to cuddle into her, and how she wished he was a more cuddly baby. As the class ended, the mother asked if anyone wanted to try on the carrier, which was green and trimmed with pink brocade.

To everyone's surprise, Darren offered to try it, and as the other students scrambled to get ready for lunch, he strapped it on. Then he asked if he could put Evan in. The mother was a little apprehensive, but she handed him the baby, and he put Evan in, facing towards his chest. That wise little baby snuggled right in, and Darren took him into a quiet corner and rocked back and forth with the baby in his arms for several minutes. Finally, he came back to where the mother and instructor were waiting and asked: "If nobody has ever loved you, do you think you could still be a good father?"

A seed has been sown here. This boy, who has seen things no child should see, whose young life has been marked by abandonment, who has struggled to the age of fourteen with scarcely a memory of love, has seen a glimmer of hope. Through these moments

of contact with the uncritical affection of the baby,
an adolescent boy has caught an image of himself as
a parent that runs counter to his loveless childhood.
The baby may have changed the trajectory of this
youth's future by allowing him to see the humanity
in himself.[6]

We can talk about compassion. But it's more likely to
be real when we volunteer with our children at a soup
kitchen or the Special Olympics, or take them to visit
a senior center or hospital. The more frequent the
visits, the more understanding will grow in children's
hearts. Instead of reacting fearfully or pityingly,
they will respond with their hearts, and respect will
follow. Lena, a teacher and writer, tells of her family
experiences:

It doesn't have to be complicated, but it's really
important to show children how to treat everyone
with respect. If you don't show them, it doesn't
matter how many times you tell them.

When we lived in Mexico, I used to work at the
shanty towns on the hills outside of the capital,
delivering medicines to people who were sick, and
just visiting around. One day my kids didn't have
school, and I brought them with me. Whenever we
stopped at someone's house, they wanted to give us
a little something, like a warm soda or juice box. The

kids could see that our hosts were offering their best. They took it with appreciation.

I want my children to be able to treat every person, no matter how rich or poor, with dignity and respect. There's a saying in Mexico, "It's better to have friends than money." Now my kids can see the truth in that.

Today even small children hear about many threatening events, from terrorism and warfare to global warming and widespread hunger. All this can make a child fearful. Here a child's simple faith in the power of good – that love and compassion are stronger than hate or indifference – can quickly transform this fear into confidence and a desire to do something for others. I have found this faith in children all over the world, regardless of their religion. But parents need to nurture it. When we tell our children that the God who made the world loves each of them personally, we give them a deep assurance that, whatever happens, they are never alone.

As a pastor, I believe that even though God and Jesus are "illegal" in public school classrooms, teachers should never be afraid to live out their faith, even if wordlessly, and let it guide their daily interactions with children. We can acknowledge and protect the spark of the eternal that lives in each of them, the

unique soul that needs our reverence and respect,
no matter how difficult or unhappy the child may
be. Children's own faith should be respected and
affirmed. If they believe that God sees everything,
that their guardian angel watches over them, or that
Jesus is their friend, this can help them withstand the
pressures that flood our culture.

There's another sphere of life that must be brought
to a child with great reverence. To me, the mystery
of birth and death can only be expressed in terms of
eternity. This is not only because of my upbringing,
since my parents lived their faith more than they
talked about it. Rather, it's because of the times in
my own life when something far greater than words
could clearly be sensed, through someone who never
spoke a word. I have seen how even the shortest life
can transform all those within its reach.

My little sister Marianne died when I was six. Our
family had waited for her arrival with great eagerness.
She was born after my mother went through a very
difficult labor for over sixty hours and suffered near-
fatal heart failure. It was miraculous that she survived
delivery at the primitive village hospital in Paraguay.
But the baby was critically ill, and only lived for
twenty-four hours. Because we lived quite a distance

from the hospital, and because I was only six, I was never able to see, touch, or hold my little sister. Still, I have felt this loss my entire life. Over time, it has become all the more important to me to remember that Marianne was – and is – a real part of my life and my family. Though she was here on this earth for only one day, she will always be my sister.

Years later, I experienced this link with heaven even more clearly through another child, my granddaughter Stephanie Jean, who will remain in my heart for the rest of my life. When Stephanie was born, we knew right away that she was a very special child with severe abnormalities. She was diagnosed with Trisomy 13, a genetic disorder characterized by a short life expectancy. Most babies born with this disorder die within a few days.

Stephanie had three sisters and one brother. They struggled to understand that their parents were not going to bring home the healthy baby they all had longed for, but an extremely disabled child who would not live long. We prayed constantly that God's will would be done in her life, and that we would grasp the meaning of her birth.

As grandparents, we experienced the wonder of holding her almost daily. Stephanie lived for five weeks, and when the time came, died peacefully. At her funeral, we could not believe how many people attended. They had all heard of her birth and diagnosis, and it affected them deeply. They wanted to participate in this last expression of love for a small child who somehow belonged to everyone.

People came from all over the neighborhood and beyond: construction workers, her siblings' teachers and classmates, the county executive, the local sheriff, and others from the law enforcement community. When the earth was shoveled by hand into her little grave, these friends and neighbors all wanted to take a turn, in an unforgettable gesture of reverence. It was remarkable how in such a short time, this little girl had touched and influenced the lives of so many people.

My granddaughter has not been forgotten. She is like a ray of light from heaven that continues to work in people and change their lives. My wife and I still thank God that he gave her to our family, and to everyone else she met.

There are many others like Stephanie. To me, every child is part of God's plan, and he does not make mistakes. When a child is disabled, her life takes on special significance. Whenever we encounter such children, we need to pay attention. They have amazing things to teach us about unconditional trust and love.

At a time when people are often assessed in terms of their worth, intelligence, or attractiveness, there are many who are not wanted or appreciated. But if we truly love children, we will welcome them all. As Jesus says, "Whoever welcomes one such child in my name welcomes me."

As a teenager I was privileged several times to meet Dorothy Day, the legendary pacifist who founded the Catholic Worker, and to participate in some thought-provoking discussions. In her bohemian days, Dorothy had had an abortion, but several years later gave birth to her daughter Tamar, and was moved to write, "Even the most hardened, the most irreverent, is awed by the stupendous fact of creation. No matter how cynically or casually the worldly may treat the birth of a child, it remains spiritually and physically a tremendous event."[7] Tamar's birth changed her mother's life, and indeed, every child has such transformative power. This is just as true of a stillborn baby, or a child who dies young.

Whether or not we believe in a loving God, we can all show love and respect toward the children in our care. This will in turn awaken their own inborn sense of reverence – both for themselves as unique individuals, and for others, just as precious and distinctive. Only then will they truly understand their purpose and responsibility in the world.

Chapter 10

Tomorrow Comes

*There are only two lasting bequests we
can hope to give our children. One of
these is roots; the other, wings.*

HENRY WARD BEECHER

There is nothing like the joy of watching
children grow, experiencing the development of their
personalities and wondering who they will become.
But as long as we have children entrusted to our care,
we cannot forget that the demands they make on us
must be answered in the present. Their name is today.
Whatever children need in the way of guidance, security, and love, they need now. Because soon enough
it will be time for them to fly on their own, and then
there will be no holding them back.
Kahlil Gibran illustrates this powerful truth:

You are the bows from which your children
as living arrows are sent forth.

The archer sees the mark upon the path of the infinite,
and He bends you with His might
that His arrows may go swift and far.
Let your bending in the archer's hand be for gladness;
For even as He loves the arrow that flies,
so He loves also the bow that is stable. [1]

How intensely each living arrow longs to travel
"swift and far"! How hard each parent must work
to remain a stable bow. It is no small thing to care
for even one child, guiding him through those first
formative years, navigating the turmoil of adolescence, and directing him toward the responsibilities
of adulthood. It seems that there are hazards on every
side. In attempting to keep their bow steady, even the
most dedicated parents can find themselves wavering
too far in one direction or another.

Ed, a guidance counselor, says that among the teens
he has worked with, the ones who slid farthest and
fastest from their parents' values were the ones who
were overprotected and never given a chance to fly:

One young man, Nick, played along with his parents
as long as he was in high school: he was a model
kid – polite and kind. But you should have seen him
once he left home – hard-drinking, sex-obsessed, and
totally unable to control himself.

Another student, Cara, felt that her parents didn't care about her as a person, but only how she reflected on them as parents. She kept her rebellion under wraps most of the time, but even then she seethed. She was convinced she'd never match their ideal of a "nice" girl, and the stricter they got with her, the more she lashed out at them. In the end, she ran off to join relatives in California, and made it clear she didn't want any further contact.

In both situations, because their parents denied them the opportunity to make mistakes, every effort to bring them up successfully ended miserably. In Nick's case, the pattern was classic: the carefully groomed child submitted as long as he had to, but once circumstances pulled him from the control of his parents, there was nothing they could do – and little he could, either, since he didn't have a foundation to stand on. With Cara the problem was familiar too: in forgetting that their child was an individual in her own right, her parents seemed to act more out of possessiveness than genuine concern, and ended up battling with the justifiable protests of a daughter who refused to be owned.

What is the alternative? To put it simply: freedom. According to my grandfather, "It is not the over-protection of anxious adults, but trust in a watchful

care beyond our power that gives a child a sure
instinct in dangerous situations. In freedom lies the
best protection for a child."[2]

Freedom doesn't mean license to do whatever one
wants. After all, we are free to drive on the wrong
side of the road, but at what cost? The youthful
desire for independence is natural enough, yet
children must be taught that it always comes with
corresponding responsibilities. To give even the most
mature adolescent no guidance at all is to ask for
trouble. As the following anecdote from my friend
Jean shows, it is also a disservice:

> I was raised in a very permissive home. This was
> intentional on my parents' part. They didn't agree
> with what they felt was repressive in the way my
> mother was brought up, and decided it would be
> quite different for their children.
>
> My father wanted me to know that there is "no
> such thing as absolute truth," and he abhorred people
> who were so narrow-minded. Once he illustrated
> his point this way: If a new bridge is being built
> connecting Brooklyn and Manhattan, it's great for
> the people who drive over the bridge but terrible
> for those who have to give up their family homes
> to make it possible. Everything is relative, good for
> some people, bad for others.

The way it worked in my life was that I could do whatever I wanted. My father said, "When you touch the stove, you find out what heat is. You will learn about life from your own experiences."

I wasn't expected to do anything around the house. My mother often complained about how messy my room was, but nothing was ever done to change it. I remember one time when I announced that I was leaving home and my father said, "OK, I'll help you pack."

I'm sure I did have some wonderful childhood experiences; it's just that the idea of childlike innocence wasn't regarded very highly in our home. If I stayed out late or didn't want to come home at night, that was okay. . . . By the time I was a young adult I had experimented with just about everything that came my way.

While many teens might regard such a lenient setting as the ideal home, Jean says otherwise. Already timid and painfully shy, the complete absence of limits or boundaries only heightened her feelings of insecurity and made her depressed:

True joy was unknown to me. I was empty inside, and desperate to find something to hold on to. Now, as a mother of teenagers myself, I have great difficulty helping them. I don't want the same void

for them. I feel their need of clear guidelines, yet I
am often simply unable to provide them. I'm still
searching for that bottom line or ground myself. It's
like I am permanently on shifting sand.

Clearly, parenting is often a balancing act, and it is as
easy to err on the side of permissiveness as on the side
of authoritarianism. To quote my grandfather again:

> Some children are brought up in an unbelievably
> free way and are, by my standards, awfully cheeky
> and naughty. But I think that too much freedom
> is better than the slavish fear that makes a child's
> parents the last ones he'll turn to. . . . Happy those
> children who have a mother to whom they can pour
> out their hearts and always count on her under-
> standing, and a father in whose strength and loyalty
> they are so confident that they seek his advice and
> help all their lives. Many people long to be such
> parents to their children, and could be, if only they
> possessed enough wisdom and love.[3]

I do not know what I would have done without the
trust my parents showed me and my siblings, even
though I know there were plenty of times when
we frustrated or disappointed them. Rather than
distancing themselves from us over those incidents,
or taking them personally, my parents used them as

occasions for deepening our relationship. My father used to tell us – and this has always stayed with me – "I would rather live in trust and be betrayed than live a single day in mistrust."

There is nothing that draws parent and child so close as such loyalty. And when I think back to the teachers who most shaped my life, I see the same pattern. Their recognition of what was striving within me – even when I couldn't express it – and their understanding of a work in progress, drew me to them in trust and confidence. I would have done anything for them.

It is rare that children cannot be reached at some level – if not by listening to them and trying to understand the reason for their silence, rebellion, or distress, then at least by acknowledging their hurt. Rules and prohibitions are seldom a help. Neither are long talks, probing questions, and attempts to make a child communicate. But respect is always in order, because it almost always inspires respect in turn. Barbara, a friend from Britain, remembers:

> One time when I was really down and tied up in knots, Dad took a day off from work and took me on a long walk through the woods, after which we had a late lunch at a country inn. He didn't try to make me

talk and certainly did not attempt to give me any kind of advice. We just spent the day together. But I will never forget that day. It really made me feel special inside.

Some time later I went through a period of real depression, and he bought two tickets for a play at a London theater. It was just me and him. . . . Looking back after all these years I'm sure he never really knew how or why I was hurting so much inside. I'm also sure that he never knew how much both gestures still mean to me.

For every child and teen, love is the greatest security we can provide. As Barbara's recollection shows, it need not even be verbalized.

Sometimes though, when it comes to building character, words are valuable. The best teachers are the ones who nudge children to ask, "Why?" and, "What can I do?" Never has the drive for uniformity in our society been more powerful. Everyone is wearing the same clothes, eating at the same chains, reading the same magazines, watching the same shows, talking about the same celebrity scandals, the same disasters, the same political events. We have been made to feel we are our own masters, but is it possible to think for ourselves anymore? Friedrich Foerster warns:

Without an ideal of personal character to fortify us, we fall prey only too easily to our social instincts; that is, to our fear of people, our ambition, our social desire to please, and all other herd instincts. Group life, the traffic of people, collective organization, and the strength and expression of public opinion, have become greater and greater, while the organization of the personal inner life has become weaker and weaker, and the true individual is smothered in the midst of all the individualism.[4]

If we are truly committed to bringing up children as individuals – to raising young women and men who have strength to defy popular opinion – we need to believe in them. The children who ask the most questions are the farthest ahead. And we ourselves can join them in asking, "Why? Why are things the way they are, and how can we change them?"

We can help children find a cause to which they can devote their energy. As we offer them the chance to give of themselves, and grow beyond themselves, they will realize that they do indeed have something to contribute. They will become aware, as Victor Frankl puts it, that the question to ask is not, "What is the meaning of my life?" but "What is life asking of me?"[5] The world is greatly in need of the change they can bring.

Raising children conscientiously, yet giving them freedom; protecting them, yet encouraging self-sacrifice; guiding them, yet preparing them to swim against the stream – all these paradoxes come together in the following story.

When Uwe Holmer was fourteen, in 1943, the patriotic teen was an energetic member of the local Hitler Youth. One day his mother found a copy of *The Black Corps,* the magazine of the SS, in his room. When Uwe came home, she took time to talk with him and begged him never to join the SS. "But, Mama, they are the toughest soldiers. They fight to the bitter end."

"Yes," she answered, "and they are the ones who shoot Jews and political prisoners. Is that the sort of organization you want to live and die for?" Uwe never forgot her question, or the look on her face.

A year later, as Germany grew desperate to hold off defeat, the army began accepting fifteen-year-olds for military service. All one hundred boys in Uwe's chapter of the Hitler Youth volunteered for the SS. Uwe refused. The leader of the group called him in and ordered him to join; his papers were filled out and ready to sign. Still Uwe refused. Next he was humiliated in front of the entire chapter, and all his privileges revoked, but he stood his ground. As he said later: "I am thankful to my mother. . . . Her courage in confronting me strengthened my conviction to live for what I knew was right."

After the war, in East Germany, Uwe married, became a pastor, and founded a Christian community for epileptic and mentally disabled adults. Over the years, the Holmers suffered repeated harassment on account of their pastoral activities, especially under the Communist government of Erich Honecker. Yet after the 1989 fall of the Berlin Wall, when Honecker fled office as one of Europe's most hated men, it was Uwe and his wife who took the ailing despot in – despite death threats and constant loud protests outside their house.

To me, the most striking thing about Uwe's story is its matter-of-factness. Yes, he had the guts to defy authority in a time and place where disobedience often cost a man his life. Years later, misunderstood and ridiculed, he withstood public opinion in defense of a broken fugitive who had nowhere to go. But Uwe's actions say as much about the power of his upbringing as they do about his heroism. And looking more closely at the source of his courage, we don't see military prowess, we see love – his mother's, and then his own.[6]

Without love, the soundest educational theory is useless, as is the most proven parenting philosophy. Janusz Korczak took a dim view of theoretical approaches:

> No book, no doctor is a substitute for one's own sensitive contemplation and careful observations. Books with their ready-made formulas have dulled our vision and slackened our mind. Living by other people's experiences, research, and opinions, we have lost our self-confidence and we fail to observe things for ourselves. Parents must find lessons not from books, but from inside themselves.[7]

This simple thought should resonate with all parents and teachers. The most strenuously outlined curriculum will do nothing for a child who feels lost, forgotten, or unloved. Conversely, the smallest act of love and confidence can carry a child across the most difficult terrain.

In the United States alone there are thousands, possibly millions, of children who do not receive the tenderness that every child deserves; who go to bed hungry and lonely and cold; who, though housed by the parents who conceived them, know little of the love of true parenthood. Add to that number the children for whom such love is denied because the cruel cycle of poverty and crime has landed father or mother or both behind bars.

The wreckage that so often passes for family life can cause people to be fatalistic about the way things are. But why should these pessimists have the last word? Dorothy Day writes:

> The sense of futility is one of the greatest evils of the day. . . . People say, "What can one person do? What is the sense of our small effort?" They cannot see that we can only lay one brick at a time, take one step at a time; we can be responsible only for the one action of the present moment.[8]

This brings a picture to my mind. A dark room is filled with people, each one holding an unlit candle. Someone enters with one burning candle and starts lighting the candles of those nearest him. Each person then turns to another, sharing the light. Within moments the whole room is aglow.

To me, this image reflects what teachers do year in and year out, without great fanfare or accolades. They ignite candles that disperse out of their sight all too soon. A good teacher will wonder about the fate of each light, or say a prayer that somewhere it is still

shining. We have to trust that these lights keep traveling outward, and that when one candle goes out,
someone else will extend their own light to kindle it
again. Parents may watch several candles out of sight.
Teachers turn from one year's lights, and ready their
flame for the next. This takes enormous reserves of
strength and love.

I am getting older; my life is coming to an end, but
I still have a great urge to use my remaining strength
to help anyone within reach, especially children.
Working in schools for over forty years, and counseling many struggling families, as well as veterans
and prisoners, I have seen much human need and
tragedy. So often, the roots of this suffering began in
childhood.

In some of the most desperate situations, I've
seen broken people rise to set right the past, asking
forgiveness for pain inflicted, and forgiving in turn
the hurt done to them. Often, they struggle hardest
to forgive themselves. Over the years, it is amazing
to see how many courageous people have overcome
violence, abuse, or alcoholism and given their children what had not been given to them.

But for every story with a happy ending, there
is another of disaster. It's as if, try as we might, our

arms are not strong enough to pull these people to safety. Surely they could have been lifted to safe ground more easily when they were children, had someone reached to do it.

If only a fraction of us are willing to commit our energy and time to helping one endangered child, many might be saved. Like every deed of love, even the smallest, most negligible act will never be wasted. Small as it might be on its own, together with others it may have power to change the world.

For whatever else might define childhood, one thing is constant: it is the gathering place of life's first and most indelible memories – the unalterable frame for all the experiences that accompany us through life. And thus in the end, the task of bringing up children is not only a question of effective parenting, and even less one of educational insights, theories, or ideals. It is, first and foremost, a matter of the love we give them, which has power to awaken more of the same, even years down the road. As Dostoyevsky reminds us in the final pages of *The Brothers Karamazov:* [9]

> You must know that there is nothing higher and stronger and more wholesome for life in the future than some good memory, especially a memory of childhood, of home. People talk to you a great deal

about education. But some good, sacred memory preserved from childhood – that is perhaps the best education. For if a man has only one good memory left in his heart, even that may keep him from evil. . . . And if he carries many such memories with him into life, he is safe for the rest of his days.

About the Author

People have come to expect sound advice from Johann Christoph Arnold, an award-winning author with over a million copies of his books in print, in more than twenty languages.

A noted speaker and writer on marriage, parenting, education, and end-of-life issues, Arnold is a senior pastor of the Bruderhof, a movement of Christian communities. With his wife, Verena, he has counseled thousands of individuals and families over the last forty years.

Arnold's message has been shaped by encounters with great peacemakers such as Martin Luther King Jr., Mother Teresa, Dorothy Day, César Chavez, and John Paul II. Together with paralyzed police officer Steven McDonald, Arnold started the Breaking the Cycle program, working with students at hundreds of public high schools to promote reconciliation through forgiveness. This work has also brought him to conflict zones from Northern Ireland to Rwanda to the Middle East. Closer to home, he serves as chaplain for the local sheriff's department.

Born in Great Britain in 1940 to German refugees, Arnold spent his boyhood years in South America, where his parents found asylum during the war; he immigrated to the United States in 1955. He and his wife have eight children, forty-four grandchildren, and one great-grandchild. They live in upstate New York.

Acknowledgments

Dozens of people helped bring this book into print. Special thanks to my wife, Verena, who tirelessly read and reread the manuscript, page after page. Without her knack for catching mistakes everyone else misses, it would be an inferior book.

Thank-you to my secretaries, editors, researchers, and proofreaders: Emmy Maria Blough, Hanna Rimes, Maureen Swinger, Else Blough, Trevor Wiser, Rhonda Johnson, Derek Zimmerman, and Sara Winter.

Finally, I'd like to express appreciation for the many who allowed me to include their personal stories in this book. It takes courage to talk about hard times; may the wisdom you shared help others along their path.

Notes

Chapter 1: The World Needs Children

1. From a radio address, Franklin D. Roosevelt, *White House Conference on Children in a Democracy*, Washington, D.C., January 19, 1940.

2. Dr. S. K. Paul, ed., *The Complete Poems of Rabindranath Tagore's Gitanjali: Texts and Critical Evaluation* (New Delhi, India: Sarup & Sons, 2006), 372.

Chapter 2: Play Is a Child's Work

1. James Hughes, *Froebel's Educational Laws for All Teachers* (New York: D. Appleton and Co., 1897), 102.

2. Edward Miller and Joan Almon, *Crisis in the Kindergarten: Why Children Need to Play in School* (College Park, MD: Alliance for Childhood, 2009), 11.

3. Valerie Strauss, "Kindergarten Teacher: My Job is Now About Tests and Data – not Children. I Quit," Washington Post, March 23, 2014.

4. Maggie Dent, "We Must Stop Stealing Childhood in the Name of Education," *Teachers Matter*, 1st edition, 2014.

5. For more about Finland's education, see: Tom Burridge, "Why do Finland's Schools Get the Best Results?" *BBC World News America*, April 7, 2010.

6. Friedrich Froebel, *The Education of Man* (New York: D. Appleton and Co., 1900), 55.

Chapter 3: Great Expectations

1. Katie Hurley, "Stressed Out in America: Five Reasons to Let Your Kids Play," *Huffington Post*, February 28, 2014.

2. Jeff Yang, "Tiger Babies Bite Back," *The Wall Street Journal*, May 14, 2013.

3. Writer and speaker Paul Tough's website: http: www.paultough.com/about-paul/qa, *How Children Succeed*, Q&A: "How did writing this book affect you as a parent?"

4. Friedrich Foerster, *Hauptaufgaben der Erziehung* (Freiburg, Germany: Herder, 1959), trans. Plough Publishing House.

5. Jessica Lahey, "Why Parents Need to Let Their Children Fail," *Atlantic*, January 29, 2013.

6. Naomi Schaefer Riley, "Dads: The Antidote to Helicopter Parenting," *New York Post*, May 5, 2014.

7. Jane Tyson Clement, *No One Can Stem the Tide: Selected Poems* (New York: Plough Publishing House, 2000), 39.

Chapter 4: Screening Out

1. Graeme Paton, "Infants Unable to Use Toy Building Blocks Due to iPad Addiction," *Telegraph*, May 30, 2014.

2. Kim John Payne, *Simplicity Parenting: Using the Extraordinary Power of Less to Raise Calmer, Happier, and More Secure Kids* (New York: Ballantine Books, 2010), 173.

3. Matt Richtel, "A Silicon Valley School That Doesn't Compute," *New York Times*, October 22, 2011.

Chapter 5: Material Child

1. For media marketing statistics, see D.G. Singer & J. L. Singer, eds. *The Handbook of Children and the Media* (Thousand Oaks, CA: Sage, 2000), 375–393.

2. Jeffrey J. Froh and Giacomo Bono, *Making Grateful Kids: The Science of Building Character* (Templeton Press, 2014), excerpt from book description.

3. Hattie Garlick, "Successful Parenting Without Spending Money: a Mother's Story," *Telegraph*, August 5, 2013.

Chapter 6: Actions, Not Words

1. Marcy Musgrave, "Generation Has Some Questions," *Dallas Morning News*, May 2, 1999.

2. Fyodor Dostoyevsky, *The Brothers Karamazov* (New York: Random House, 1950), 383.

3. Barbara Kingsolver, "Either Life is Precious or It's Not," *Los Angeles Times*, May 2, 1999.

4. Malcolm X, *The Autobiography of Malcolm X* (New York: Ballantine Books, 1987), 411.

5. Trent Toone, "Ravi Zacharias Discusses the Bible, His Life, Families, and Religious Freedom," *Deseret News*, January 18, 2014.

Chapter 7: Guidance to Grow

1. Dorothy Law Nolte, *Children Learn What They Live: Parenting to Inspire Values* (Workman Publishing, 1998), *vi*.

2. Betty Jean Lifton, *The King of Children: The Life and Death of Janusz Korczak* (New York: St. Martin's Press, 1997), 80.

3. Anthony Bloom, *Beginning to Pray* (Mahwah, NJ: Paulist Press, 1970), 5.

4. The Editorial Board, "Giving Up on Four-Year-Olds," *New York Times*, March 26, 2014.

Chapter 8: In Praise of Difficult Children

1. For Ritalin statistics, see: http://www.pbs.org/wgbh/pages/frontline/shows/medicating/drugs/stats.html

2. From Peter Breggin's March 29, 2000 interview with epidemiologist Michael Savage, posted on NewsMax.com.

3. YouTube: Temple Grandin, "The World Needs All Kinds of Minds."

4. Carl C. Gaither and Alma E. Cavazos-Gaither, eds., *Gaither's Dictionary of Scientific Quotations,* 2nd edition, (New York: Springer, 2012), 483, 1956.

5. Thomas Lickona, *Raising Good Children* (New York: Bantam Books, 1994), 125.

6. Steven McDonald, NYPD detective and speaker for Breaking the Cycle, first introduced "You Are Very Special" to our staff. The original text was written by a group of students.

Chapter 9: Discovering Reverence

1. Herman Hesse, *Vivos Vocos,* March 1919, as translated and quoted by Eberhard Arnold in *Salt and Light* (New York: Plough Publishing House, 1997), 48.

2. Diane Levin, *Beyond Remote-Controlled Childhood: Teaching Young Children in the Media Age* (Washington DC: NAEYC, 2013), 16, 37. Copyright © 2013 National Association of the Education of Young Children®. Reprinted with permission.

3. Helen Handley and Andra Samelson, eds., *Child: Quotations about the Delight and Mystery of Being a Child* (New York: Penguin Books, 1990), 74.

4. Eberhard Arnold, *Children's Education in Community* (New York: Plough Publishing House, 1976), 13–14.

5. Erich Maria Remarque, *The Road Back* (Fawcett Publishing, 1998), 252–255.

6. Gordon, Mary, *Roots of Empathy: Changing the World, Child by Child* (Toronto: Thomas Allen Publishers, 2005), 5–6.

7. Stanley Vishnewski, comp., *Dorothy Day: Meditations* (Newman Press, 1970), 10.

Chapter 10: Tomorrow Comes

1. Kahlil Gibran, *The Prophet* (Eastford, CT: Martino Fine Books, 2011), 26.

2. Eberhard Arnold, *Children's Education in Community* (New York: Plough Publishing House, 1976), 23.

3. Eberhard Arnold, from an undated letter (probably October 1908) to his fiancée, Emmy von Hollander, trans. Plough Publishing House.

4. Friedrich Foerster, *Hauptaufgaben der Erziehung* (Freiburg, Germany: Herder, 1959), Plough Publishing House translation.

5. Viktor Frankl, *The Doctor and the Soul: from Psychotherapy to Logotherapy* (Vintage, 1986), xxi.

6. Uwe Holmer's story has been reported in books, magazines, and on the internet. The direct quotes are translated from Thomas Lackmann, "Beim Abschied umarmten wir uns" (an interview with Uwe Holmer), *Der Tagesspiegel,* Beilage Weltspiegel Nr. 16860.

7. Janusz Korczak, *Loving Every Child: Wisdom for Parents* (New York: Workman Publishing, 2007), 1.

8. Dorothy Day, *From Union Square to Rome* (Preservation of the Faith Press, 1938), 127.

9. Fyodor Dostoyevsky, *The Brothers Karamazov* (New York: Random House, 1950), 938.

Index